Code

Be Codependent No More and Overcome Anxiety in Relationships through attachment theory, Boost Emotional Intelligence and Self-Confidence, Take Back Your Life After Narcissistic Abuse

Lesanka Bogoevski

Table of Contents

Introduction

For many people, it can be frustrating going through a series of failed relationships and dysfunctional situations in their lives. If you have been on the receiving end of toxic relationships, this may be the right time and place to find a solution to the emotional baggage that may be holding you back. Codependency is not uncommon nor is it a life sentence. There is a way to recover and find your way back to healthy relationships.

You may have experienced codependency first hand or watched a friend or family member go through it. In either of these situations, the toll that codependency takes on both relationships and individual well-being is enormous. Unfortunately, it can be easy to mistake codependency for a series of bad choices or more commonly just conclude that you are unlucky when it comes to relationships.

That is why the first part of this book is dedicated to helping you identify if you are codependent. It helps you self diagnose by going into detail into the codependency characteristics that may be plaguing your relationships without you being aware of what they mean. The most important aspect for recovery to occur is to first realize that you indeed have a problem.

My research into codependency was inspired by watching a close friend endure perpetual emotional turmoil as she struggled to detangle herself from a toxic relationship. Codependency goes beyond just relationships between addicts and their enablers. It is a far-reaching condition that can affect anyone in any kind of relationship. From parent to child relationships, love relationships and even friendships there is always potential for negative emotional attachment to occur.

In this book we have therefore taken a wholesome approach to codependency, exploring it in all its different aspects and spectrums. Your situation does not have to mimic the classic addict-enabler dynamic to fit within the codependency spectrum. You will be surprised to find that you may be in a codependent relationship and have been oblivious to your emotional dependency tendencies.

Self-discovery is often uncomfortable, but only by identifying and accepting your flaws can you hope to get past them. This book is intended to help you face your innermost and deepest unresolved issues. It may be difficult digging deep into a dysfunctional childhood but you can only unburden yourself by taking apart the emotional baggage you may have been carrying with you for years.

This book first seeks to help you identify where your codependency triggers may originate from and where you are most vulnerable. From this background, the book then charts a course through recovery techniques that will help you overcome codependency and break away from the destructive shackles of emotional dependence and dysfunctional relationships.

If you have often wondered to yourself, *how did I get here* or *why am I this way*. You will be able to trace your unresolved issues back to their origins and understand how best to resolve them. From this foundation, we then take an in-depth look into the process of recovering from codependency. This book takes you through effective techniques that will help you to recover from codependency and establish better and healthier relationships.

If you are looking for a quick fix, this book is not a magic wand that will wipe all your emotional baggage away overnight. It is a practical guide full of useful strategies and tools for people who want to have better relationships and break away from codependency. It is meant to provide you with tools to empower your recovery from codependency that you can go back to time and time again.

If you have been trapped in toxic relationships and cannot seem to find your way out, this book is intended to help you identify and detach from narcissists and energy vampires. We understand that information is only useful if you have the tools to use it. Each section in the book that addresses the recovery process from codependency is packed with practical tips that will help you in everyday life.

Whatever challenges, hurts and unresolved issues you carry as a result of codependency, recovery is not just possible but within your reach, if you are willing to follow the techniques in this book.

If you are ready to chart a new path for yourself and detach yourself from dysfunctional relationships, this book is intended for you. The best place to start is in the beginning; understanding what exactly codependency is.

Chapter 1: What is codependency?

Jenny's Story

She is sitting with her head down as if by looking down she can somehow negate the grim reality that has her sitting in the sterile hospital waiting room at 3 am. The squeaking soles of medics walking by in urgent purposeful steps are hard to ignore. She is waiting anxiously for news on Matt and nobody seems to have any news for her just yet. She sits in a semi daze bracing for the worst and fervently praying that he is alright.

At some level, the call at midnight was not surprising. Jenny had been divorced from Matt for just over three years but she was still his emergency contact. It caused some friction between her and Dave, her current partner, but she seemed helpless when it came to walking away from the father of her two children. Divorced or not, their lives were permanently linked.

Matt had spiraled after their divorce. Drinking, gambling and even occasionally doing drugs in an attempt to cope with the separation from Jenny and the boys. Jenny knew enough not to blame herself, but she still felt responsible for him. His parents were long gone and his two siblings did their best to stay away from him and New York in general. That left Jenny, for better or worse, she was his lifeline and boy! did he use it often.

Jenny was not oblivious to how dysfunctional this dynamic was. It had become the main fighting point in her relationship with Dave. On some level, she was almost certain that Matt would be the thing that broke her and Dave up. He was tired of being part of the dysfunctional threesome dynamic that still tied Jenny to her ex and had him constantly intruding on their life.

Dave's exasperation was growing and he had asked Jenny more than once to just cut off the apron strings and move on. If only it was that easy, she would have done it in a heartbeat. Matt was the father of their two sons and at the very least she could take care of him for their sake. Jenny had primary custody of the boys, but their eyes lit up every time Matt came to see them. So, for them, she was in a hospital waiting room, on a Tuesday night at 3 am, waiting.

The gambling had started before the divorce, but the rest of the vices had piled on like dominoes falling in quick succession. It was classic escapism and, on some level, Jenny understood it. Matt had been a doting father and being separated from his children seemed to have broken him in some fundamental way.

In the three years since they had parted ways, Jenny had rescued him from jail after a DUI, taken him to the emergency room after an accidental overdose and even paid off numerous gambling debts. So, no, the call at midnight had been no surprise.

His upstairs neighbor in the apartment complex where he lived is the one who had called. He had found Matt passed out cold on the stairwell. Matt had been unresponsive and the neighbor had called 911 before calling me. All he knew was that they had taken him to St. Martins down the road.

She had rushed to the hospital, still in her pajama bottoms and petrified of what she would find. Dave had been angry at the intrusion in the middle of the night. He had asked her not to go, but in the end, they both knew she had no choice. She had to see that Matt was alright. So, she left in a rush, mind working a mile a minute, hoping fervently that the father of her children was not dead. Anything but that.

> *How many scars do we justify because we love the person holding the knife?*
>
> Anonymous

No matter where you go, there you are. This old adage is a rather apt description of the inevitable fact that we cannot escape who we are. Have you noticed how life sometimes seems to unfold in patterns? You keep ending up in the same situation you swore would never happen again. You fall in love with the same person you broke up with just with a different face. In effect, your life starts to feel like reruns of a rather old movie with a broken record.

Let's take relationships for example. It is not uncommon to find that all your relationships tend to take on a similar trajectory. Every time you think you have found "the one", the same issues that sunk your previous relationships start to crop up and you end up at the same place you started only with a lot more emotional baggage.

This continuous loop is down to the inevitable fact that the one thing that remains constant is you. You carry your emotional and psychological baggage with you and like it not, every experience in your life good or bad is tainted with this baggage. So naturally, if we cannot escape ourselves, the next best thing is to become self-aware.

Ever thought to yourself why do I always attract needy people? Or how come everyone in my life is so judgmental? We often think that it is people who choose to treat us a certain way, yet have you ever considered that they are simply responding to your personality or emotional state? Have you ever stopped to wonder what part you play in the outcome of your relationships?

It is a simple law; the path of least resistance is usually the easiest to take. The people around you are drawn to the bits of you that complement or validate them. So naturally, if I like being cared for, I will seek out someone who loves taking care of people. If I am egocentric, I will want to surround myself with people I can control.

These natural predispositions to be attracted to or attract certain types of people are so intrinsic in our natures that they happen almost at a subconscious level. Think of a narcissist who wants to be the center of attention at all times. It is highly unlikely they will want to be in a relationship with a fellow narcissist. After all, these are two self-absorbed personalities that cannot fulfill each other's need to be the center of the universe.

They will instead seek out someone who can cater to their needs and focus all their attention on making the narcissist happy regardless of their own needs. In this case, the perfect match for the narcissist is almost always a codependent person. But what exactly is codependency?

Codependency is the need to be approved and validated by others emotionally psychologically and physically. Codependents place their focus on someone else's life and draw satisfaction from making the other person happy or content. For a codependent, other people's needs come before their own and they are not happy unless they feel needed, or approved by the people in their lives.

Codependents will over function or do more than is necessary for other people's lives while doing very little or under-functioning in their own lives. Codependents find themselves in unequal relationships where they are the perpetual giver and the other person just takes without giving anything back.

The reason that codependency can have such far-reaching effects in your life is partly due to the fact that there is nothing overtly wrong with loving other people or wanting to take care of them. In fact, relationships are built around love, so what is so wrong about putting the needs of other people before your own?

Well, for codependents, the line between caring for others and enabling them is thin and often non-existent. This is driven by the fact that a codependent person thrives on approval from others. This means that as codependent even when you are sacrificing for others, you are getting satisfaction from their neediness and dependence on you. And what can be more addictive than a self-replenishing drug?

Let's go back to the beginning of the chapter and consider Matt's situation. Here is a divorced man who constantly relies on his ex-wife to put his life back together for him. Obviously, he gets a free ride for all his shortcomings and there is no reason for him to give up the relationship. But what's in it for Jenny who is putting her relationship at risk to go to the rescue of her ex-husband? Is it all just empathy or is there more?

People who are not codependent, know when to draw the line and create boundaries. This is because even when they care for others, they still retain a sense of self-worth that drives them to take care of their own needs. In contrast, for codependents, the needs of the other person surpass their own wellbeing. This means that they will do what it takes for the other person regardless of the consequences to their own lives.

In Jenny and Matt's case, she needs to be needed and gets satisfaction from being the hero that always saves Matt. This is not only detrimental for her but also, in the long run, damaging to Matt. Jenny is doing what most codependents do; enabling the abuser to continue self-destructing or harming others. This is the real danger of codependency.

At its core codependency is driven by the refusal to acknowledge a problem and seeking to restore control or order by sacrificing for others despite the consequences.

Think of a mother who will give her son just one more pill so he can feel better or a woman in an abusive relationship who stays because her husband will be lost without her. In this case, the enabler is doing more harm to the other person by giving in but they cannot help themselves because of their need for approval and control.

As a codependent when you are enabling someone else, you feel good because in the short term they will be grateful. You thrive on the other person's approval and feel that if you just make everything okay for them then all will be well. However, what you do not realize is that you are as addicted to their approval as they are to their vices.

How Does Codependency Develop

Codependent traits tend to develop early in life. As a child you are at your most impressionable and the environment in which you grow tends to shape your personality. In dysfunctional families, children tend to develop traits that predispose them to become codependent adults.

Dysfunction does not always refer to physical abuse. It is any situation in which a child feels emotionally neglected, unsafe or unworthy. If you have codependent tendencies in most cases you developed them in childhood. Some common examples of environments that could have made you codependent include:

- Overly judgmental parents who made you feel like you cannot do anything right
- Poor stability in the home that made you feel unsafe or insecure
- Neglectful parenting where your parents were inattentive
- Manipulative situations where you were made to feel guilty or ashamed constantly
- Overly harsh parents that you were eternally trying to please and placate

In any one of these scenarios, the bottom line is you start to develop traits to help you cope in the environment in which you find yourself. If for instance, your parents were neglectful or unable to take care of you, you will find that you develop caretaking tendencies.

When you become a caretaker, you want to take on the responsibility of making sure everyone else is okay. This is the most common trait in codependents. This caretaking behavior makes you put the needs of others before yours. If as a child no one took care of your needs, then you ended up having to be the responsible one who takes care of everyone.

In the case of the child growing up in a judgmental environment, it is natural for them to become a people-pleaser who is always trying to get approval from others. If you find you have a constant need to be approved by others, your codependency may stem from a dysfunctional childhood where you had to work hard to get any approval from your parents or caregivers.

Guilt is a common driver of codependency and like all the other traits, this one may be traced back to a childhood of feeling responsible for the dysfunction in your family. Children in broken homes often feel like they are the cause of the problems in their family. If you grow up in this kind of environment you are likely to develop guilt-driven codependency where you feel responsible for other people's problems.

Most codependents develop a tendency for being control freaks. This may stem from the fact that you often felt helpless and insecure as a child. As a result, you developed the need to control situations and people around you so that there is some order in your life.

Fear is also a common driver of codependency. The fear of loss, the fear of failure and the fear of being alone are common triggers of codependency. These insecurities are planted in childhood in dysfunctional environments. You will find that you are afraid of being alone so you will do anything to keep the other person happy. These fears are what create enablers who in trying to repair and hold on to relationships push the other person to do more harm to themselves and others.

Children are stuck in the environments they find themselves in. You did not choose your family any more than you chose to be born, this means that if you developed codependency traits, they were simply as a coping mechanism to deal with the situation you found yourself in. Blaming yourself for your personality is not only a waste of time but wholly unproductive.

Although your childhood codependency traits may have followed you into adulthood, that does not mean you are stuck with them for good. Once you acknowledge the problem, then you take back power over your life and start the journey to healthy relationships.

Characteristics of Codependency

Perhaps you have recognized some of the traits we have mentioned above in yourself. But does that necessarily mean if you are a caretaker or a people pleaser you are codependent? In most cases, codependency is not just one of those things but a combination of traits that hinder you from having healthy and happy relationships.

Here are the main characteristics of codependents:

a) Over functional in other people's lives.

You take responsibility for other people's problems and needs while neglecting your own.

b) People-pleasing.

You need constant approval from others and will do anything to make others like or love you.

c) Controlling.

You want things to work a certain way because it gives you a sense of order. You are prone to telling others how to do things and when to do them.

d)Low self-esteem.

You have a low sense of self-worth and you need other people to make you feel good about yourself.

e) Self-defeating.

You ignore your own needs and give priority to other people's wellbeing.

f) Martyr-complex.

You feel the need to save or rescue others even if it comes at a cost to you and your needs.

g) Anxiety and depression.

You repress so much of your feelings and they start to fester and manifest as anxiety and chronic stress.

h) Prone to emotional outbursts.

You lose it over small things because you tend to let resentments and anger fester until you cannot control yourself anymore.

i) Intimacy issues.

You have problems opening up to people because you do not trust them not to hurt or disappoint you.

j) Emotional contagion.

Your feelings of happiness or anger are dependent on what the other person is feeling. If they are happy you are also happy and if they are anxious you become stressed.

You may have one or more of these characteristics depending on where you fall on the codependency spectrum. For many codependents, the net result of these character traits is they find themselves constantly feeling emotionally drained.

Codependents travel with a lot of emotional baggage. Imagine if you had a grocery bag and all you could do was fill it in, and never take anything out. At some point, it will start bursting at the seams because it cannot hold anymore. This is what codependency does to your emotions and psychological state. It overburdens you and makes it impossible for you to have healthy relationships.

Relationships require give and take in equal measure, and if all you are doing is giving, at some point you will run out. This is the reality for many codependents who find themselves in a continuous cycle of dysfunctional relationships.

Different Types of Codependency

The Hero

Codependency is not a one-size-fits-all personality type. It comes in different forms and one of the major ones is the hero complex. This type of codependent is a perfectionist and control freak. They probably had narcissistic parents and grew up taking care of other people's needs and being praised for it.

The codependent hero wants to save other people or rescue them. They need to feel in control by taking charge of situations. In our case study, Jenny is a classic example of a codependent hero. She rushes to the rescue every time Matt has a problem because she feels that if she takes control everything will be all right.

At their core, heroes are seeking approval and validation from others. They are rescuing someone not just to help them but also to feel good about themselves and their capabilities. Heroes tend to be ambitious and overachievers. They strive for perfection in their lives and are in constant pursuit of it.

If you are a hero codependent you often find people coming to you for help. You feel that you are the only one who can fix a problem and that if you do not, the world will fall apart. You tend to take on other people's problems and ignore your own needs.

While composed and centered on the outside, the hero carries the weight of other people's problems and is often stressed, and emotionally drained.

The Scapegoat

The scapegoat codependent is driven by guilt and shame. If you are in this category, you were probably the problem child at home. You got into lots of trouble in school and was always up to mischief. This type of codependent has been dealing with blame and being shamed for most of their life.

In their attempt to overcompensate they become the eternal scapegoat always blaming themselves for other people's behavior. Let's look at a classic example, the woman in an abusive relationship. Have you ever wondered what would make them stay even when they are being emotionally and physically abused? In most cases, it is because they feel that on some level, they deserve the punishment they are getting.

This type of codependent has very low self-esteem. They feel that they need to make up for their mistakes or shortcomings by letting the other person treat them any way they please. If you are this type of codependent, you have problems speaking up for your self or letting other people take responsibility for their actions.

Scapegoats tend to suppress their emotions and minimize problems. They are prone to addictions and often engage in self-destructive behavior as an outlet for their repressed emotions. Relationships for scapegoats are difficult because they are unable to articulate their emotional needs.

The Invisible Child

For codependents who grew up being ignored by their parents and not getting attention from them, the common coping mechanism is the invisible child complex. This type of codependent learned in childhood that their needs are unimportant because nobody paid attention to them.

If you fall in this category you are likely to be introverted and most comfortable in solitude. You have trouble being intimate with others because you do not know how to be in a healthy relationship. You grew up having no attention and have become accustomed to self-isolating and disconnecting from others.

If you are an invisible child type of codependent you often find that you have problems with intimacy in your relationships. You will often feel disconnected in your relationship and your partner will have a hard time understanding you because you are so poor at expressing yourself.

The Caretaker

The caretaker is an enabler. If you are in this category, you probably grew up in a dysfunctional environment where you needed to take care of others. You have a martyr complex and believe that you need to solve other people's problems and fix their lives.

The caretaker thrives on being needed and feeling useful. They go above and beyond to make the other person happy; consequences be damned. This is probably why behind every addiction or self-destructive vice is an enabler trying to keep the addict happy.

Caretakers are unable to recognize that the other person has a problem. They feel it is their responsibility to fix the other person's life. If you are a caretaker codependent you often end up in relationships with damaged people who you think you can save.

Caretakers or enablers are often the most harmful of codependents because, in their attempt to save the other person, they cause more harm than good. If you are an enabler, fear is probably one of your driving factors. You are afraid of losing the other person so you choose to help them self-destruct just to keep them happy.

Enablers combine the hero complex with a sense of martyrdom. If you are a caretaker you have the need to be needed in order to feel purposeful or worthy.

Are you Codependent?

Self-awareness is often not as easy as it sounds. We often operate on autopilot and rarely take the time to examine our emotions and behavior. You may be codependent and not know it. In fact, since codependency has a lot to do with loving and caring for others, you probably think that your relationships are healthy.

So how do you know that you are codependent? Here is a simple quiz to guide you.

i.   Do you get lost in relationships and take on the persona of the other person?

ii.   Do you stay in bad relationships because you are afraid of being alone?

iii. Do you always find yourself in unequal relationships where you are always the one trying to keep the other person happy?

iv.   Do you always say yes to others even when you disagree or do not have the time or means to help them?

v.   Are you constantly sacrificing your needs to make others happy?

vi.   Do you constantly feel the need to take care of the people in your life and fix their problems?

vii.   Is it hard for you to make decisions in a relationship and always defer to your partner?

viii.   Are you always concerned with other's people opinions and getting their approval?

ix.   Do you feel bored or useless if you are not taking care of someone?

x.   Are you uncomfortable when others try to help you?

xi.   Do all your relationships tend to end the same way?

If you answered yes to less than 5 of these questions you have some codependent tendencies which do not necessarily make you codependent.

If you answered yes to 5 or more of these questions, you have a codependent personality.

Chapter 2: Codependency and Relationships

In Greek mythology, the tale of Narcissus is a well-known fable. The nymph Echo falls in love with Narcissus who is by all accounts an astonishing beauty. Unfortunately, for the lovelorn Echo, the self-absorbed Narcissus is too in love with himself to have much room for anyone else much less the nymph Echo.

In pursuit of her great love Echo follows Narcissus into a forest. She is determined to declare her love and win him over. Echo takes her chance and calls out to him. Narcissus, however, has no use for her and turns away from Echo, leaving her to call out to him in despair. Echo spends the rest of her life pining for Narcissus, withering away in this state until there is nothing left of her.

In a deserved twist of fate, Narcissus does not fare any better. He dies while contemplating his beauty in a pool from which he cannot tear himself for fear of losing sight of his reflection. Naturally, this tale of woe is used as a lesson to caution the selfish and the self-absorbed. It is used to portray the self-destructive power of narcissism.

But what about the hapless Echo, who is nothing if she can't be with Narcissus? Isn't hers also a cautionary tale for those who base their existence solely on the approval of others? Is she just a victim or just as responsible for her fate as Narcissus is?

While the tale is mythical, there is no illusion to the fact that narcissists will always attract codependents. Like a moth to a flame, codependents often find themselves falling for the self-absorbed narcissist whose only true love is the reflection they see in the mirror. In this way, the slow burn begins and, in the end, all that is left of the codependent is an empty husk that is all tapped out.

Narcissism and Codependency: The Unholy Union

Opposites attract, that is just the way nature works. In most cases, this is a great thing, after all, every yin needs its yang. For instance, if you are neurotic and high strung, a composed and emotionally balanced person will make a perfect partner for you because they will balance you out. If you are introverted and end up in a relationship with an extrovert you will likely find that you start to open up more and more.

Opposites bring out the best in each other by complementing each other's strengths and flaws. This is true in most cases unless of course, we are talking about a narcissist and a codependent. Far from being ideal, the codependent – narcissist union is quite literally a match made in hell. But who exactly is a narcissist?

The simple definition of a narcissist is a self-entitled person who places their desires, needs and feelings above those of others. A narcissist is incapable of empathy because they cannot understand or contemplate needs or feelings beyond their own. Narcissists need to be the center of attention and demand that everything is done their way.

24

Narcissistic personalities abound in society. Most of us have that one friend who is never happy until things are exactly the way they want. They want you at their beck and call at any time, yet they are rarely there for you if you need them. They ask you to do things for them that they would never do for you if the tables were turned. Narcissists are the reason we find ourselves in toxic friendships, relationships, and even families.

If you interact with a narcissist on a personal level, at work or even as an acquaintance, if you are not codependent, you are likely to survive these toxic relationships largely unscathed. However, for codependents who are unable to take care of their own needs and establish boundaries, their relationships with narcissists are damaging and have long term effects on their emotional and psychological wellbeing.

At their core, narcissists and codependents have more similarities than you may think. Both these personalities are driven by the need for approval, a need to control others and dependency on others for validation. What separates the two is that while the narcissist wants to control others to get what they want and meet their own needs; the codependent wants approval and to feel useful by being overly functional in other people's lives.

Think of it this way, if we go back to our case study, Matt is the classic narcissist. He has no qualms intruding on Jenny's life whenever he needs help or to be saved from some mishap or other. Jenny, on the other hand, is a codependent who thrives on being needed and taking control of other people's life. Essentially these two people are dependent on each, but for two very different reasons. One has selfish goals while the other needs the validation they get from being the rescuer.

This toxic dependence is what makes narcissists and codependents often end up together. They satisfy each other's need for approval and validation but in different ways. When a narcissist finds a codependent, they know that they have found someone who will always be at their beck and call no matter what. On the other hand, codependents find a sense of purpose in being needed by the narcissist.

But what could go wrong in such a union? After all, if they complement each other's needs so well don't they sort of deserve each other? Unfortunately, no, the relationship between the narcissist and a codependent is not only destructive to both parties but doomed to fail from the start. Whether the narcissist in your life is a parent, spouse, child or even friend, for a codependent this is one relationship they need to get out of and avoid all costs.

Of course, if it was that easy, then there wouldn't be a problem. Why do codependents find it so hard to leave toxic relationships with narcissists? This is partly because narcissists are masters of manipulation and have perfected the art of laying traps for codependents.

Traps narcissist lay for codependents

a) Shame

There is probably no other personality as adept at using shame to control others as the narcissist is. Narcissists know that codependents are people pleasers who need the approval of others and this makes them the perfect victims for shaming. Shame is an effective tool for control because it makes the codependent want to make up for their shortcomings by doing whatever the other person wants to keep them happy.

If you have grown up with a narcissistic parent then you are no stranger to being shamed into things you did not want to. In narcissistic family situations, phrases like: *look what you made me do..., you are so ungrateful..., what will people think..., look at how you have hurt so and so..., why are you so selfish..., do it for the sake of the family...* are the order of the day. A narcissist will use shame to control a codependent and justify their own actions.

Now imagine someone who grew up being shamed consistently and being made to feel sorry for every little action that their parent did not agree with. Chances are this person becomes codependent as an adult and is susceptible to being controlled using shame. As we discussed in the first chapter, traits that become entrenched in childhood are hard to break in adulthood.

Shame has kept many a codependent in an abusive situation simply because they feel they are getting punished for something they deserve. If you are a codependent person in a relationship with a narcissist, you will often find yourself feeling ashamed and wanting to make up for your shortcomings, real or imaginary, by letting the narcissist control what you do, feel and even think.

*"if you hadn't done this then I wouldn't have had to..., am only doing this to protect you..., you would look so much better if you..., you never do anything right..., it's your fault....*If you often hear these types of phrases in your relationship, it may be time to re-evaluate whether you are being manipulated.

b) Low self-esteem

It is hard to control someone with healthy self-esteem and a sense of self-worth. Naturally, a narcissist does everything in their power to make you feel worthless. From criticizing how you look, your outfits, your weight, your career choice and everything in between. A narcissist has one goal, to make you feel you are not good enough and that you need them to make your life better.

Ever had a friend who would make cruel jokes about you in front of others and enjoy when people laughed at you? When you told them later how you felt about it, their defense would always be, *lighten up it was just a joke.* This is one of the classic ploys' narcissists use to break down your self-esteem. They are experts at putting you down both in public and in private.

If you grew up with a narcissistic parent, you were probably always being compared to a "better" sibling or relative. Constantly being told how *if only you could be like so* and so or *why can't you do it the way so and so does it.* These criticisms not only undermined your self-esteem but preconditioned you to thinking that other people are better than you in some way.

If you carry this low self-esteem into adulthood then you become the perfect victim for a narcissist. This is because you already think very little of yourself and the narcissist only has a short distance to go to convince you they are better than you.

A narcissist needs you to think there is nothing special about you so you can devote all your attention to them and catering to their needs. Codependents in relationships with a narcissist will often get lost in the relationship and lose all sense of their personality, likes and dislikes because they are constantly being critiqued.

A codependent in a relationship will slowly start changing how they dress, speak and even their friends. This is because they have been told their choices are wrong in some way by the narcissist. As a result, the codependent starts to strip away bits of themselves little by little until they are a completely different person.

You may have a friend who completely changes when they are in a relationship. Or you may be the codependent whose personality changes depending on who you are with. While it is not unusual for people to rub off on you and make you want to be a better person, if you often feel the need to change who you are in order for a relationship to work, you may be a codependent being manipulated by a narcissist.

c) Envy

Have you gone from a completely normal and emotionally balanced person to an obsessive and jealous version of yourself you barely recognize? Narcissists are masters of making you feel jealous and insecure. They want you to make them the center of your universe and devote all your energy to protecting and guarding the relationship.

A narcissist will flirt with other people in your presence just to make you feel envious. Narcissists understand that most codependents need to be in relationships to feel whole. They exploit the codependent's fear of being alone by making them feel envious and insecure. You are more likely to ignore someone's faults if you are scared of losing them and narcissists know this only too well.

If you are in a relationship with a narcissist you will find yourself constantly feeling insecure. You will start doing things you previously thought only crazy people do. Going through your partner's phone, becoming clingy and needy, always suspecting your partner is cheating and emotional outbursts become the order of the day.

Envy breeds insecurity which in turn lowers your self-esteem even more. Of course, there is a certain level of jealousy even in healthy relationships. However, if envy consumes you to the point that all you think about is what your partner is doing, who he is with or whether he might leave you, then you may just have fallen into a narcissist's trap.

Ultimately, narcissists exploit a codependent's weakness to the point where the codependent is helpless and unable to leave. The power of narcissists over codependents is not just in their ability to lay emotional traps, but also the fact that they can easily suss out codependent personalities. Once they have established your need for approval, all the narcissist has to do is lay a trap and you are sunk.

Understanding the Attachment Theory

Humans are not built for solitude. From a young age, we thrive on attachments and bonds to others. A child becomes emotionally bonded to the parent and caregivers even before they learn how to speak. This is because emotions are an integral part of the human experience. We feel things even before we can understand them because emotions are powerful and inevitable.

How we attach to others is primarily at the root of the kind of relationships we have. Out attachments styles determine the nature of our relationships and how healthy and unhealthy they are. These attachments styles are formed early in life and like personality traits, they follow us into adulthood.

Secure attachment

Secure attachment is the healthiest form of attachment. If you fall into this category, you have healthy self-esteem and are able to relate with others on the grounds of mutual give and take. You have a well-developed sense of self and even when in a relationship, you still take time to take care of your own needs.

While you do enjoy being in a relationship, you are also equally happy on your own and do not need the validation of a partner to feel complete. You find yourself often in fulfilling relationships that are nurturing. It is easy for you to resolve conflicts and get past misunderstandings because you are able to manage your emotions and understand other people's.

Secure attachment stems from a stable childhood where a child felt adequately cared for and nurtured. They were able to express themselves freely and had emotionally responsive parents. This healthy upbringing resulted in an individual who is able to articulate their needs in a relationship while also being considerate of their partner.

If your attachment style is secure, you will rarely fall prey to narcissists or toxic relationships. This is because, from a young age, you have developed a clear understanding of what a healthy relationship is and what it isn't.

Anxious attachment

Like the name suggests this attachment style is fraught with insecurity and fear. If you have an anxious attachment you are most likely codependent. You find yourself in relationships where you are the giver and the other person is the taker.

You are constantly trying to please the other person and keep them happy. This is despite your own needs. You pay very little attention to your own emotional wellbeing because you are so preoccupied with making the other person happy. In this kind of attachment, your happiness is tied to making the other person happy.

You do not do well alone and will often find yourself hanging on to dead and toxic relationships just to avoid being alone. You find yourself often being referred to as clingy and needy. This is because at the base of all your relationships, lies the fear of being abandoned or left alone.

If your attachment type is anxious, you most likely grew up in a dysfunctional situation. Emotional neglect, abuse, controlling parents, and addiction situations in childhood are some of the hallmarks that lead to anxious attachment. The lack of healthy relationships in childhood means that even as an adult you often find it difficult to have healthy relationships.

Codependents have this attachment style. They put the needs of their partner before their own and can become compulsive about keeping the relationship no matter the cost. If you have an anxious attachment style, most of your relationships tend to be dysfunctional. You are often unhappy in your relationships but too scared to leave because you do not want to be alone.

Avoidant attachment

In this type of attachment, the recurring theme is emotional detachment. If you have this attachment style you shy away from commitment. You will probably jump from one relationship to another, always finding a reason to leave before things get serious.

You find yourself being paranoid that the other person is trying to change or control you in some way. You are the kind of person who will leave a relationship because the other person is too tall, laughs too loud or whistles in the shower. Anything or more accurately nothing is enough to break your relationships because at your core you want to avoid emotional attachment at any cost.

Most people with avoidance attachment often had dysfunctional relationships in childhood. They grew up having to protect themselves from being hurt and disappointed by others. The easiest way to do this is, of course, avoiding emotional connection. This is what followed them into adulthood and laid the groundwork for avoidant attachment.

If you have this type of attachment style, you will always find yourself ending relationships for petty reasons. You are afraid of commitment and most of your partners never really know what you are feeling because you have a hard time opening up emotionally.

It is important to note that these three attachment styles can change. Someone with a secure attachment can be triggered into an anxious attachment by the kind of partner they choose.

Similarly, someone with an anxious attachment can change if they get into a healthy relationship with someone who is not manipulative or abusive.

You are not doomed to stay anxious or avoidant all your life. Once you have identified where your issue lies, then fixing it is only a matter of dedication and knowing how. For codependents shifting from anxious attachment to secure attachment starts with self-awareness and self-acceptance.

How Does Codependency Affect Your Relationships?

Codependency has often been referred to as a disease. This is because much like any other disease, codependency is a reaction to a situation that is off-kilter and it is progressive. Consider a codependent who is enabling a person with an addiction such as alcoholism. The sicker or more addicted the addict becomes, the more compelled the codependent feels to help or enable them.

Codependents are the proverbial ostrich that buries its head in the sand. For them, it is difficult to acknowledge that the other person has a problem. They try and fix things for them by providing instant gratification which only allows the problem to fester and grow. Like any other habit, enabling is a hard one to break because when you become so accustomed to doing something it starts happening almost on a reflex level with no conscious thought involved.

Let's go back to Jenny's story at the beginning of the book. She is so used to rescuing Dave that when the call comes at midnight her first and only reaction is, *I must go see him*. While of course, it is natural to want to look after the people you love, consider what would have happened if Jenny had said no any of the previous times when Dave had called for help.

In all likelihood, had Jenny told Dave no the first time he messed up, he would have known that he is responsible for the consequences of his actions. This means he would not have gotten away with so many other misdeeds after that. In essence, providing an addict with a lifeline only gives them leeway to get even worse. This is why codependency or enabling is as harmful to the victim as their drug of choice.

Codependency affects you, your partner and ultimately your relationship. Like we said at the beginning of chapter one, most codependents will often find that their relationships follow the same trajectory. If you feel like you are on a continuous downward loop going nowhere fast in your relationship, this may be because codependency is affecting your relationship.

Here are the main ways in which codependency affects your relationship:

i.   You become controlling. You want to follow every detail of your partner's life because you are unable to focus on your own needs.

ii. You are jealous. You become hypervigilant about monitoring your partner because you are always coming from a place of fear. The fear of being left or abandoned.

iii. You have a problem with boundaries and you will often overstep the other person's space emotionally and physically.

iv.   You do not have a separate life of your own. You always want to follow your partner everywhere because your whole life revolves around them.

v.   You often sacrifice your needs to make the other person happy even if it hurts you.

vi.   The main reason your relationships fail is that the other person feels suffocated or smothered.

vii. You are prone to emotional outbursts because your suppressed emotions tend to erupt. You find yourself overreacting to petty and trivial things.

viii. You are seldom happy in your relationships.

Warning Signs Your Relationship is Codependent

Relationships, even at their best are hard to navigate. It is impossible to have a completely problem-free relationship where everything is just rainbows and butterflies. Outside of fairytales, relationships take work and a commitment to making things work to flourish.

So how do you tell if you are in a codependent relationship or whether you are just having normal relationship problems? Fortunately, the distinction is not hard to make. Codependent relationships are easy to identify because, in these kinds of relationships, everything that can go wrong often does.

Here are the major warning signs that point to a codependent relationship.

i.   You have lost yourself in your relationship. You have trouble identifying how you are feeling, what your needs are and anything else that does not involve your partner.

ii.   You are constantly giving in to your partner. Your relationship is about you pleasing your partner. You rarely get your own way.

iii.   You take on your partner's responsibilities. Whether its something as simple as bills or bigger things like raising your children, you always end up doing what your partner should be doing.

iv.   The weight of keeping the relationship alive falls on you. You are the one always planning romantic getaways, surprising your partner and ensuring their needs are met. You are rarely ever on the receiving end of romantic gestures or thoughtful gifts.

v.   You are in a constant state of anxiety. You are always worrying about how your partner is feeling, whether your relationship will work and whether you are good enough.

vi.   You often feel emotionally drained and resentful because your needs are seldom met.

vii.   You are in a relationship with an addict of some kind. You always seem to attract or end up with people who are damaged and then take on their problems for your own.

viii.   You allow physical, emotional or psychological abuse in your relationship. You often feel put down, humiliated or ashamed yet you feel powerless to leave.

ix.   You often cancel your own plans so that you can do what your partner wants.

x.   You cannot recall the last time you actually felt happy or content in your relationship.

Chapter 3: Codependency and Addictions

Jenny's Story

Matt did not die; in fact, he was out of the hospital in a little over a week. He had taken a concoction of drugs and alcohol that had overwhelmed his system. He would probably have choked on his own vomit and died if the neighbor had not found him when he did.

If there was a silver lining to the whole mess. It was that it had not been a suicide attempt, just a drunk doing what he does best. When discharging him, the kind doctor at St Martin's recommended a rehab center for Matt. On the drive home from the hospital, Jenny pleaded with him to consider rehab, if not for his sake then for his two sons. In the end, he agreed to go albeit halfheartedly.

The rehab was a welcome relief. Dave and Jenny finally had time to focus on their relationship without constant interference from Matt. They started mending their relationship and everything was back on an even-keel in no time. She had never realized just how much intrusion and strife Matt caused in their lives until those Matt-free months when he was safely tucked away in rehab.

Jenny found freedom in knowing she could go about her business without constantly dreading the next midnight call from a hammered Matt in some kind of trouble. Seth and Collins bonded so much with Dave that they stopped asking when their daddy was coming to visit. Dave was good with them and they grew to love his steady presence in their life.

This bliss lasted for about four months. On a beautiful sunny day when Dave and Jenny were grilling steaks out in the back for the boys, Matt showed up. He was unshaven, disheveled and obviously drunk. He told them that he had been kicked out of rehab a few weeks back. It did not take him long to get back to his old ways and he had since then spectacularly fallen off the wagon.

Matt told Jenny that he was there to see Seth and Collins. In his drunken state, she could not allow him near them. This set him off and he lost the little composure he had. Dave had to threaten to call the police when Matt started yelling and throwing things. He claimed that they had no right to stop him from seeing his sons. Dave was equally adamant that he would not see them in his sorry state. After what seemed like an eternity of yelling and shouting, Matt finally gave up and left.

In the middle of this melee, Jenny could see Seth and Collins peering outside from the windows. They looked scared and confused. It broke her heart to think of what it must be for them to see their father in that state. She was struck by the selfishness of a man who would put his kids through that kind of pain repeatedly and never take any responsibility for his actions. That scared look on her boys' faces is what brought Jenny to her senses.

She decided that she was going to yank the lifeline. She had given so much of her life to protecting Matt that in the process she had let her children down. Jenny realized that she was in a healthy relationship with Dave but she was still jeopardizing it in a misguided attempt to save her ex-husband from himself.

She knew it would not be easy to finally let him go but she had tasted freedom in those four Matt-free months. This glimpse of what the future could be like if she ended the toxic relationship would be enough to motivate her through the change.

She still wished him all the best but he would no longer be welcome in her life. She was done.

The Link Between Substance Abuse and Codependency

It is no coincidence that most substance abusers are in relationships with codependents. This is because the substance abuser needs someone to enable their habit and help them meet their needs. And who better to fill those shoes than a codependent who is a natural people-pleaser?

In a healthy relationship, if a person in your life starts abusing drugs or any other substance, you are likely to call them out on it and push them to seek help. Whether it takes tough love, denying them money or even having them go through rehab, a person who is not codependent will recognize the problem, acknowledge it and takes steps to stop it.

Sadly, when it comes to codependents in relationships with people with substance abuse problems the reverse is true. Most codependents have a hard time acknowledging the other person has a problem. They will focus on trying to make the other person feel better. For instance, it is not unusual to find a codependent married to an alcoholic actually purchasing alcohol for the addict.

Codependents become enablers of addictions because on some level they may feel guilty or responsible for the other person's actions. They do not know how to let the other person take responsibility for their actions so they shoulder the blame. In doing this, the abuser gets leeway to manipulate the codependent into giving them their drug or substance of choice.

It then becomes a vicious cycle where the abuser is manipulating the codependent and the codependent is trying to keep the abuser happy. The net result is that the addiction spirals out of control because no one in the relationship is addressing the actual problem.

Think of a single mother raising a teenage boy who starts doing drugs in his teens. The teenager will probably have problems in school and in their home but the mother will always think *if he had a father, he would not be like this.* In this scenario, the mother has assumed the blame for her son's actions and the worse he gets the more she will blame herself.

Even when he starts selling off stuff from the house to support his habit, she is unlikely to seek outside help. This is because she has already made up her mind that he is not responsible for his actions. So, in this case, the most likely outcome is that the boy will eventually end up graduating to crime to support his habit or he will end up dead in a gutter somewhere from an overdose.

Scenarios like this are why codependents in relationships with addicts are a danger both to themselves and the substance abuser. Codependents not only help the abuser get worse, but they themselves are prone to developing addictive tendencies to cope with the dysfunctional situation.

Enablers do not have to be spouses or partners, they can be mothers, children, siblings or even friends. Imagine a child who has grown up with an alcoholic parent. They most likely have to take care of their parent and younger siblings when the adult is unable to do so. This child is likely to become codependent because they are used to taking care of everyone. This is partly why children who have parents with substance abuse issues are likely to become enablers.

If left unchecked, codependents can sometimes be the death of the addict in a very literal sense. This is because they valiantly cover up any substance abuse problems until it is too late. It is not unusual to hear a codependent making excuses for their partner in public. They are dedicated to keeping up the façade that all is well.

This makes the situation even more dangerous for the abuser since people on the outside are kept unaware of the problem. Sometimes by the time other friends and family know there is a problem, the situation is too far gone to salvage.

Enablers may have good intentions but by enabling the addict, they take away the opportunity to seek treatment or help. They undermine efforts by others to help the substance abuser by providing a link between the addict and the substance.

In most cases both the addict and the codependent need to seek treatment to break the cycle of codependency and substance abuse. It is also important to realize that codependency can develop as a result of being in a relationship with an addict.

You can start a relationship with a completely healthy person. After a while, if this person starts to develop an addiction you will find yourself thrown into the role of an enabler. Many codependents are well-meaning people just trying to save the person they love.

However, if you feel the need to cover up your partner's abuse problems, find yourself buying drugs or alcohol for them or making excuses for their behavior, you are creating a dysfunctional enabler-addict dynamic.

Enabling an addict doesn't necessarily mean that you are scoring drugs for them. Anything that jeopardizes the addict's chance of recovery or makes it easy for them to access their drug of choice is enabling. The best way out of this cycle is through getting professional help for both the addict and the codependent.

If we look at Jenny's story at the beginning of the chapter, she realizes that as long as she is providing a lifeline for Matt, he has no chance of recovery. The only way out is for her to completely cut him off and let him get the help he needs. This is the realization that most codependents need to come to. An addict will always stay hooked provided there is someone there to pick up their slack.

Codependents and Enabling Behavior

It may seem pretty straight forward – if someone is abusing drugs or other substances simply stop supporting them. For most codependents leaving a relationship is not that easy. You will find that a codependent can enable an addict for years and years. This begs the question, what makes codependent so susceptible to becoming enablers?

Here are the main factors that make codependents prone to enabling behavior.

a) Lack of boundaries

If you are codependent, you have trouble separating your needs, responsibilities, and emotions from those of other people. This means that in a relationship you cannot separate your partner's problems from your own. So, if you get into a relationship with an addict you treat their problem as if it is your own.

This lack of boundaries is what drives you to enable the addict because you are unable to hold them responsible for their own actions. You take it upon yourself to fix their problem and in this way give them the leeway to keep abusing their substance of choice. After all, no one is holding them accountable so what reason do they have to stop.

b) People pleasing

This is one of the primary causes of enabling behavior. Codependents are naturally people-pleasers who will do anything to keep the other person happy. In the case of a codependent–addict relationship, this usually means that the codependent will help the addict access drugs or other substances if that is what they want.

The need for approval is strong enough to make the codependent cross lines that they would never do in normal circumstances. There are many people in jail right now because they fell in love with someone with a drug problem and got caught up in the mess.

All enablers are people-pleasers and find it difficult to say no to the other person. They will go against their values, sacrifice their needs and even break the law to keep the other person happy.

c) Shame

Remember the scapegoat type of codependent we discussed in chapter one? Well, this type of codependent is a classic enabler. Shame is a powerful motivator and it can make a codependent do anything to make up for their mistakes or shortcomings.

An enabler may feel ashamed because they blame themselves for the addict's problem. They feel that in some way they may have pushed the addict to abuse drugs or other substances. The codependent therefore takes on the role of enabler to assuage their shame and guilt.

In most cases, addicts also know how to use shame to manipulate the enabler into helping them. They make the codependent feel that it is their fault the abuser is addicted and therefore they should do everything to keep the addict happy.

d) Control

Enablers need to be needed. This type of codependent enjoys the sense of control that they have over the person who needs them, in this case, the addict. Addicts rely on the enabler heavily since most of them are not very functional in their day to day lives. This neediness gives the enabler a sense of control and power.

Enablers get a sense of purpose from knowing someone needs them. They thrive on being the person the addict can turn to for help. Enablers who are driven by a need for control are the most dangerous because since they are happy to keep the addict unwell for as long as possible.

e) Fear

Fear is almost always a common denominator in a codependent's life. The fear of losing someone they love. In the enabler's case, this person is the addict. If the addict is only with you because of their habit or addiction, it stands to reason that if they got better, they probably would not need the enabler.

This fear of becoming irrelevant or no longer useful to the addict is what keeps the enabler in a position of aiding the addiction.

Think of a pimp who uses drugs to control his girls. If he gets them hooked on drugs, they will need him for more than just protection, they will be reliant on him for their daily fix. This buys him loyalty and as long as he can keep the girls well supplied, they will keep working for him.

Are you in Denial?

See no evil, hear no evil. This seems to be the enabler's creed. To understand how denial works in codependent relationships to foster addictions, let us look at abusive relationships. When we think of addictions it is natural to think of substance abuse and diseases like alcoholism. But addictive tendencies cover a wide spectrum including violent behavior.

Women who stay in violent relationships are enablers. They make it possible for the abuser or the perpetrator to resort to violence. Statistics show that a huge majority of domestic violence cases go largely unreported. But what would make someone subject themselves to violence over and over again?

While there is no single answer to explain this, one of the main tools that people use to enable domestic violence is denial. Denial is a powerful drug and most people who practice it make a habit of it. It becomes their safety net when they cannot understand or process what is going on.

A woman being abused by a spouse will find a million and one reasons not to confront the actual problem which is the partner's violent tendencies. Instead in their head, they will look for alternatives to explain or even justify why they are being abused.

They will choose to think *oh he was just having a bad day...,or he was drunk..., or I did not cook it the way he likes it..., or it was my fault....* All these excuses are just their way of refusing to face the reality that they are married to a monster. Denial then becomes their go-to hiding place whenever things go wrong.

In the classic sense, if we look at enablers in terms of addictions, we will see that though the situation is different from domestic violence, the main theme is the same. Refusal to acknowledge the existence of a problem. The only way an enabler can keep aiding an addiction is if they are in denial about how grave the situation is.

The enabler will tell themselves things like: *he only needs to get past this rough patch..., just one more pill then she will be ok..., it is just a beer it doesn't matter.* In this case as well, the enabler reasons their way out of resolving the situation by minimizing the problem and denying the gravity of the situation.

If you have codependent tendencies you have to be on the lookout for the tendency to be in denial. Are you consciously or unconsciously ignoring problems to avoid upsetting your relationships? Denial can be your biggest downfall because it is pretty hard to fix a problem that you have not acknowledged.

So, what are some of the signs that you are an enabler in denial?

1. Do you often find yourself making excuses for other people's actions a behavior?

2. Are you always defending your partner from other people?

3. Do you always need to cover up for other people's shortcomings in public like doing their work for them?

4. Do you encourage your partner to only rely on you and try to shield them from other people?

5. Are you constantly trying to fix things for someone else?

6. Have you given someone help in terms of money or other resources knowing fully well they would use it for their addiction?

This simple self-examination will help identify if you have a tendency to make excuses to avoid facing the reality of a problem.

The Path of Least Resistance

When it comes to going against the current or riding the wave, the choice is always simple. We follow the path that comes easily to us because, at the end of the day, familiarity breeds comfort. Even simple routines like what time you wake up in the morning, once they catch hold, become hard to break.

If you wake up at 6 am every day in the morning. You will find that it becomes so ingrained in your brain that you do not need an alarm to wake you up. It simply becomes a natural habit. Similarly, when it comes to addictions, we often find that changing long-held habits is well near impossible.

For both the codependent and the addict, the patterns of behavior they have established become almost second nature. Breaking this pattern, therefore, becomes as difficult as trying to paddle upstream in a fast-moving creek. Just like any other habit, when it comes to codependency your emotions and brain travel the familiar path.

This means that if you do not make a concerted effort to change and break the pattern, you are likely to ride the wave of codependency to destruction. If you have carried your enabling and caretaking tendencies from childhood, into adulthood it means that you are so accustomed to thinking a certain way that you might as well be operating on autopilot.

We said at the beginning of the book that life tends to unfold in patterns. This is simply because our behavior and emotions remain the same over time. If you have always needed validation from others to feel content in a relationship. You will carry this need into every relationship you get into. This means that all your relationships will have the same trajectory.

This constant circling back on a seemingly endless emotional roller coaster can make you feel helpless to stop this pattern of dysfunction in your life. However, like any other habit, codependency is not a life sentence. It can be broken and broken effectively.

Let's look at a different habit, let's say binge eating. If you wanted to stop this habit what would you do? Naturally, you will start by analyzing what triggers your binge eating episodes. Do you binge eat when you are anxious? Do you binge eat when you are stressed? Do you binge eat when you are with your friends?

Once you identify your trigger, let's say its stress. Then you know that every time you are stressed you are likely to binge eat. So, a possible solution would be looking for a different way to de-stress, let's say yoga or exercise. If you slowly implement this change the less dependent you will be on binge eating for comfort.

This is just to say that the easiest way to break bad habits is to create new and better ones. In the case of codependency and addictions, for example, you can train yourself to start by learning to say no. If your partner asks for money to buy alcohol or any other substance just say no. Of course, the first few times will be hard but the more you do it, the easier each subsequent no becomes.

The point is to break the pattern of behavior and create a new one. This is the easiest way to escape the slippery slope that is the relationship between codependency and addiction. By taking small but decisive steps each day to free yourself from the role of an enabler, you will find yourself feeling free from the burden of being responsible for someone else's problems.

In Jenny's case, she found the strength to break free from her need to protect her children. This is what spurred her on to make the change from enabling an addict to focusing on living a happier and better life. Find your own turning point and dig deep to understand what codependency is robbing you of on a daily basis and make the choice to take it back.

Sometimes in the story of your life, you have to be willing to be your own hero. You have got to decide that you want a better life, that you deserve a better life and that you shall have a better life. No one can decide that for you, but once you do the rest is easy.

Chapter 4: A New Beginning

> *Saying NO to the wrong things creates space to say YES to the right things.*
>
> Mack Story

As far as love stories go Romeo and Juliet had it pretty rough. I mean what's the point of all that love if all it does it take you to the grave? Of course, for romantics, the sacrifice was the ultimate expression of love. However romantic it may be, you really do not want that to be the story of your life.

Self-emollition in real life for the sake of a relationship only ends one way. With a broken heart and in some cases long term psychological damage. If you are tired of your relationships reading like a Shakespearean tragedy minus the romance and the love, maybe its time to turn the page.

Despite all fairy tales to the contrary, the only person who can complete you is you. A relationship is not meant to become an extension of you but rather a union between two people, each complete in their own right.

So now that you have discovered that you have codependency tendencies where do you start? How do you go from having all your self-worth tied up in someone else to being a whole person?

Well, let us start at the beginning; you.

The Power of Self Awareness

If you are codependent, chances are, you are so caught up in other people's lives you hardly know where you stop and where they begin. In fact, one of the most common symptoms of codependency in relationships is that you get lost in your relationships.

You forget what used to make you tick, what your needs are and even what your goals are. You get so preoccupied with the other person's needs that every time you look in the mirror you barely know the person looking back at you. It's the ultimate loss; losing yourself to hang on to someone else.

Let's consider Susie's situation. Susie was a happy go lucky young woman, always vibrant, happy and confident. She had lots of friends, a great career and her life was pretty much on the up and up. Susie is introduced to Jack by a mutual friend and before long Susie and Jack are not just an item but inseparable.

Everyone is happy for Susie, after all, she is a wonderful person who deserves to be happy. Slowly, however, happiness turns to worry because Susie starts to withdraw from her family and friends. She is all of a sudden always unavailable even to her own parents. She spends all her free time with Jack and has no time for her friends and family anymore.

The few times they do manage to coax her out, the once happy Susie is now a somber and distant person her friends barely recognize. The personality change is so obvious that the friends know that something is wrong immediately. Sadly, Susie insists all is well and all her friends can do is watch their friend wither away.

Relationships have a way of changing us, the good ones make us better while the bad ones destroy us. This is especially true for codependents who have a problem with boundaries and self-awareness. If you have a poor sense of self-awareness then it becomes even harder to understand if a relationship is changing you. You need to first know who you are before you can be in a healthy relationship.

How can someone else love you if you have no idea who you are? Self-awareness goes beyond knowing whether you are a cat person or a dog person. It has more to do with understanding yourself, your values, interests, emotions and even your triggers. It means being able to say at any given point that *I am feeling this way and this is what has made me feel that way* or *this is what I want for my life and I know how to get it.*

It sounds simple enough but you will be surprised at how many times we have no idea how we are feeling much less why. For codependents who spend their lives caught up in other's people's needs, self-awareness is even harder. If you are codependent, it is not surprising to find yourself often feeling anxious or stressed without exactly knowing why.

This is because as a codependent, you have spent most of your life suppressing your emotions and feelings. As a codependent, you are always the giver in the relationship so you never get asked what you are feeling or what your needs are. It is, therefore, no surprise that codependents are much more adept at reading other people's needs and emotions than they are at understanding their own desires and needs.

Self-awareness is simply getting to know yourself. Identifying what your core values are, knowing what you want out of a relationship and all the other bits and pieces that make you complete. The importance of cultivating self-awareness is that it is almost impossible to extricate yourself from codependency if you have no idea who you are.

How can you tell if your needs are being met in a relationship if you have no idea what those needs are? The reason codependents' moods are dictated by their partner's emotions is due to the fact that they are unaware of their own feelings and therefore just mirror what their partner is feeling. This means that if your partner is happy, you will be happy and if they are not you will mimic their anxiety.

While narcissists may thrive on this kind of environment. A healthy person will immediately shy away from being in a relationship with someone who cannot express themselves. Lack of self-awareness can damage the health of your relationships. Nobody wants the burden of being responsible for their partner's moods. If all you are doing is mirroring your partner's emotions, you are likely to drive them away. A strong sense of self is an attractive quality to have and healthy relationships need a healthy balance between two equal partners.

Think of a child when they are at a young age. They are unabashed about expressing their needs. They cry when they are sad and laugh when they are happy. They let you know what they want and demand your attention when they feel you are inattentive. Somewhere along the way we lose this childish innocence and learn to suppress our emotions.

This constant suppression is what takes us farther and farther away from understanding our own needs and feelings. Think of it this way, if you are always working hard to maintain a façade on the outside, you will likely lose touch with your inner self.

So how exactly do you cultivate self-awareness? How do you go from being a sponge that simply soaks up the persona of your partner to be an independent and whole person in your own right?

Getting to Know Yourself

Self-awareness is the ability to recognize your needs and emotions. It involves knowing how you are feeling at any given point and more importantly why you are feeling that way. Behind every emotion, there is a trigger and once you know what your triggers are, then you will have better control over your emotions.

For instance, if you find that you are a people-pleaser who constantly needs validation from other people. How did you get there? What insecurities make you feel that way. By using self-analysis, you can discover truths about yourself that may help you break the chains of codependency.

Self-awareness goes beyond just understanding your emotions. Here are the key areas you need to focus on in your journey to self-discovery.

a) Values

Having core values is key to being an independent and balanced individual. Values shape your behavior and choices in life. Values are like the moral compass you have inside your head that tells you where your true North is. We all have values that we have formed over time.

One of the key ways in which codependents lose their sense of self is that they usually put their values aside to adopt those of their partner. For instance, if you believed in being kind to strangers and you get in a relationship with someone who doesn't. You will find that you slowly lose your empathy for others because as a codependent you are trying as much as possible to reflect your partner's values.

The key danger of losing or suppressing your core values is that you become reactive in nature. Since you have no guiding principles of your own, you start instead just reacting to things as they happen. This makes you more likely to make bad choices and engage in destructive habits.

Holding on to your values is one of the most important things you can do to reinstate your sense of self and independence as a person. Look back to who you were before the codependent relationship. Did you value honesty, commitment, loyalty or trust? Were you close with your family, what kind of relationships did you yearn for? and so on.

These kinds of self-analysis questions will help you identify what your values are. Ideally, you should write them down starting from what is most important to you. For instance, if you value trust above anything else you can have that as your number one value and then list down the rest.

This simple exercise is helpful in helping you to build your self-awareness. You start to realize all the things you may have compromised on in your codependent relationship. Understanding your values is a key step in reclaiming your sense of self and discovering what matters most to you.

b) Interests

For codependents, their lives revolve around their partners and they seem to have no personal interest or hobbies of their own. However, if you dig deeper you can discover things that are interesting to you and things that you are passionate about that have nothing to do with your relationship or other people

Think back to a time before the relationship, what did you enjoy? Music, art, reading or simply taking walks in nature? The activity is not important, what is crucial is for you to identify the things that interest you and that you enjoy doing. If you have spent most of your time doing what other people want, this is the time to spend time on your own hobbies and interests.

Develop interests outside of your relationship that have nothing to do with your partner. If you love discovering new places, take a trip by yourself and enjoy your hobby. If you love cooking, take a cooking class to expound on your hobby. Whatever activities that you are curious about, make an active effort to engage in them regularly.

The more you explore your hobbies and interests the more you will find that you are capable of having fun on your own without relying on someone else to make you happy. If you cannot think of any hobby, do not fret, try a new activity every week until you find something you enjoy doing.

You can take a yoga class this week, visit a museum the next week, volunteer at a children's home the next and so on and so forth. Slowly you will start to realize that you are creating a life for yourself that is independent of relationships or other people's needs. The more you explore the more you will discover things about yourself you never knew.

The same way you dedicate your time to other people's needs, take that much time and devote it to your own passions and interests. People are drawn to people who have their own goals and interests and a semblance of a life. Developing yourself on this level will only make your relationships better. You may have heard the phrase many times but **Get a Life** never gets old, it literally means start living.

c) Temperament

Do you know your temperament? Are you an extrovert, introvert, a little of both? Having an idea of what your disposition is, puts you in a better position to know what is working in your life and what is not.

Let's say for example that you are a planner by nature. You like things organized and done in a certain way. Now if you constantly put yourself in disorganized and chaotic situations then you will always be in a constant state of anxiety. This is because your environment goes against your inner nature and therefore you are never quite at ease.

If you are a codependent who is not able to express your needs, you will often find yourself in situations that go against your disposition. If you are an introvert and your partner happens to be an extrovert, unless you are able to express this to them, you might end up in a lot of uncomfortable situations.

There is nothing wrong with being with someone who is your exact opposite provided you can articulate your needs. Once you are able to say, *I would rather spend some time indoors this weekend*, then you and your partner can arrive at a compromise. His needs can be met on the days you go out and socialize while yours can be met on the weekends you choose to stay in. This is a healthy give and take dynamic in normal relationships.

On the other end of the spectrum is a codependent who instead of telling their partner they'd rather not go out, will follow their partner with a smile plastered on their face. This suppression of your needs will only fester and brew resentment in your relationship. Its no wonder then that codependent relationships seldom work because one person is going against their nature to please the other.

Take time to find out what your inner self thrives on. Are you spontaneous, controlled, uninhibited, or any other trait that comes naturally to you. Once you discover what your temperament is, you can then make informed choices on what is and what is not good for you. Don't just go along to get along. Having an understanding of your own disposition is part of having a well-developed sense of self.

d) Life goals

When you were a child you were probably pretty confident about what you wanted to be in the future. Teacher, doctor, astronaut, zookeeper, clown, whatever your chosen future self would be, you would say it with no hesitation to anyone who would ask. Maybe it changed every week but you certainly had a notion of what you wanted your future to be like.

What happened in between to make you lose this ability to have a dream or a goal to aspire to? Whatever it was, you need to go back to having some goals and aspirations for yourself. No matter how small or humble, goals give you a reason to get out of bed in the morning. They give you purpose and build up your self-esteem.

Remember in chapter three we discussed how enablers slip into this role as a way of finding purpose for themselves? Goals are an effective way of finding purpose outside of your relationship. If you are codependent you need to start setting goals that are not about your partner or your relationship but about yourself. Start small if the idea intimidates you.

Set a goal to achieve by the end of the week. It can be as simple as cleaning out your closet or as major as signing up for classes for a course you have always wanted to take.

The whole point is to find something for you to not only look forward to but that will also make your life better. Set weekly goals for yourself, then slowly build up to monthly and long-term goals. Imagine if you had a quiver of arrows and a bow but had nothing to aim at. There wouldn't be much of a point to having them would there?

Goals give you something to shoot for. They set a path for you to follow and help you to discard all the little bad habits you have picked up to fill up your days. If all you do is over function in your partner's life, the best way to shift focus back to your own life is by setting goals for yourself.

Sit down with a notebook and think of what you want to accomplish in a week, a month and even a year from now. Be brutally honest and only focus on goals for yourself. Your goals cannot be about someone else or their life. They have to be about you, your dreams and your needs. This step will bring you ever closer to becoming self-aware and an independent being that is not codependent on others.

e) Strengths

Human beings are all flawed in some way. However, none of us is so flawed that they have no strengths. We all have things we are good at and those are basically your strengths. Are you a good cook, are you a great writer, do you have an uncanny ability to empathize with people? No matter how small you think it is, you have strengths that make you who you are.

When you know your strengths then you know exactly what you bring to the table. Let's consider the biblical David and Goliath. On one corner we have this giant Philistine, battle-trained and physically indestructible. On the other hand, is a small teenage boy who has never fought anyone in his life. So how did David beat this mammoth?

Well for starters, he did not go out and try and wrestle with this giant because obviously, physical strength was not where his advantage lay. Instead, he used what he was good at. He had a slingshot and he knew how to use it. So, a small boy defeats a trained soldier with nothing more than a slingshot and a couple of stones.

You do not need to be a Christian to understand the moral of this story. It is really not about the battle in itself but about knowing where your strengths lay. When you understand what you have that you can use to make your life better, then you no longer need to seek validation from others. Understanding your strengths arms you to face the world and whatever challenges life has to throw at you.

If you have caretaking tendencies from childhood, that's great. It doesn't have to be a bad thing. You can use that to volunteer in a care home or look for a profession that allows you to take care of others. Playing to your strengths increases your chances of success significantly. The confidence boost you get from excelling is just a bonus.

Self-analysis will help you suss out your strengths. List them down. If you are having a hard time, try thinking of something people always compliment you on or notice about you. At the end of it, you will start to realize that you have more strengths than you think. Focus on these strengths and work out how to tie them into your goals.

Dropping the Shame, Guilt, and Blame

For codependents, shackles do not come any tighter than shame, guilt, and blame. You wear these scars like a battle-scarred soldier that cannot escape the ravages of war without realizing that it is these three things that hold you hostage to codependency.

We talked about how narcissists and addicts use shame, guilt, and blame to manipulate codependents. This technique is so effective that all a narcissist has to do is to shift blame and the codependent is back to trying to make everything alright again.

If you are to break free from codependency these are the primary weights you need to eradicate from your life. The hardest part about ditching guilt, blame and shame is that these are in most cases traits that you carried with you from childhood. This means they have become so entrenched in your life that you are hardly aware that your codependency is being driven by shame, guilt, and blame.

We often confuse shame and embarrassment but we need to make the distinction between the two. Embarrassment is what you feel in the presence of other people. Let's say you made a dismal presentation at work and your boss chastises you in front of your colleagues, what you feel in such a scenario is embarrassed.

Shame has more to do with what we think of ourselves. If you, for instance, have an addiction you may sometimes feel ashamed of yourself and not want people to find out about it. You may think it makes you look stupid or weak or any other negative way. The point is, shame is what you feel about yourself and your perceived weaknesses and shortcomings.

Shame is, therefore, such a powerful force because it is internal. No one can take it away from you but you. Internalized shame taints everything you do including your relationships. It makes it possible for codependency to thrive because you are always trying to make up for the things you are ashamed about.

Guilt and blame, in much the same way as shame, allow you to become codependent by clouding your better judgment. If you are in an abusive situation and all you can see is that you are somehow to blame for your partner's violence, you are unlikely to seek help or even get out of the relationship. Guilt makes you feel that every bad thing that is happening to you is somehow deserved and therefore you have to take it.

People in dysfunctional homes are always feeling guilty about what is going on around them. Think of a child whose parents are getting divorced. If this child starts feeling responsible for the parents breaking up, this guilt is likely to make him codependent. He will always carry the burden of guilt and feeling responsible for everything that goes wrong whether or not it is actually his fault.

When you have a combination of guilt and shame already, then blame is not too far behind. You will find it easy to take the blame for other people's actions. An enabler living with an addict will often find themselves thinking that addiction is their fault. This makes it harder for them to say no to the addict because on some level the enabler feels they need to solve this problem because it is their fault.

If you succumb to shame, guilt and blame you can end up in a never-ending cycle of codependency that taints all your relationships. It is therefore imperative that you first look at all the ways that shame, guilt, and blame make you codependent.

These are classic signs that shame, blame, and guilt have made you codependent.

i.   You always feel responsible for other people's problems

ii. You self-sacrifice to keep other people happy no matter how it makes you feel inside

iii. You often find yourself covering up for other people's mistakes

iv. You have trouble saying no even when you know it's the right thing to do

v. You never express your own needs or feelings and simply go along with what the other person is saying

vi. You value the opinion of others more than you value yourself

vii. You are prone to emotional outbursts and have depressive tendencies

If any of the above traits are a constant in your life then its time you become free of shame and guilt. This is only possible if you are willing to uncover the root of your shame and unmask the hidden feelings that make you feel this way.

Here are everyday tips you can use to minimize the role of shame, guilt, and blame in your relationships.

1. Explore your motives

The first thing to dropping shame is to analyze your motives. This means going behind your actions and behavior to see what your end goal is. For instance, if you said yes to an addict. Ask yourself why? Why did I give him the money to buy drugs? Is it because I want him to be happy? Did I want to feel better about myself? Did I want him to be grateful? If you find the answer to why then you have found your motive.

If you find your motives have nothing to do with helping the other person or solving the problem, then you can now fully understand that your actions are simply being driven by shame, guilt or blame. So every time before you make a decision or choice in your relationship first analyze your motives.

The more you learn to analyze your motives, the better you will get at weeding out bad decisions that are made based on guilt or shame. This step is especially important if you find yourself playing the role of an enabler or codependent caretaker.

2. Accept your past

You cannot make up for bad decisions in your past by living your life trying to make up for the guilt you feel. Accepting that the past happened and that you cannot go back and change it is a crucial step in healing yourself.

Life is happening now and getting caught up in all your past mistakes simply robs you of your future. Learn to let go. If this is hard for you. Try writing a letter to yourself. Write down all the things you did wrong. Acknowledge that they happened, apologize for them and give yourself the right to move on.

There is something freeing about simply writing down your past and getting all the negative thoughts out of your system. Not only is it therapeutic but it also gives you the chance to put things in perspective. Ever noticed how big a mistake can seem if you just think of it as this big event that happened? However, if you break it down into small pieces it starts to seem manageable and surmountable.

Whatever it is, big or small, your past mistakes will only have power over your future if you let them. If you are having trouble shaking the past, find support. Therapy is a safe space to share your thoughts and get the past out of your way. Reach out to close family and friends and talk to them about the things in your past that haunt you.

You will be surprised how even just talking about it lightens the load of your past and enables you to break free from it.

3. Imagine a new reality for your life

Codependency is emotionally and physically draining. Your needs are always on the back burner because you are too busy fulfilling other people's needs. So why don't you imagine what it would be like to be free of all your self-imposed burdens and responsibilities?

There is a reason vision boards work and it has nothing to do with magic. Envisioning a better future not only gives you something to work towards but also helps you focus on what you want. So, create a vision for your life without codependency.

Imagine yourself in a healthy and happy space where you are not constantly trying to get approval and validation from others. Freeing, isn't it? Now take an image that gives you that feeling of freedom and pin it to your vision board. Look at it every day in the morning and in the evening and remind yourself that that is where you want to go.

Envisioning a different life for yourself makes it easy to say no to things you no longer want in your life. Slowly you will find that you are carving out a path to the freedom you envisioned. In life, it is the small choices that we make daily that get us to where we need to be.

4. Learn from your mistakes.

Do not let your past mistakes go to waste, learn from them. Life is not perfect by any stretch of the imagination so learning to accept your flaws is part of self-acceptance. So, what if you have been divorced three times? It only means you are three times wiser than you were when you first started. It means that next time you will have the experience to know better and do better.

Every mistake shows you which path to avoid the next time. Instead of carrying around guilt and shame from what you did or did not do, chalk it up to experience and promise yourself that you will do better. Once you accept your mistakes and forgive yourself for them, use them as valuable life lessons to better yourself.

Wisdom often comes with age. This is simply because the older you get the more mistakes you have made and learned from. Do not be too hard on yourself for making mistakes in the past. The only thing you can change is the future and the present and the best way to do that is to learn from the past.

Practicing Self-Empathy

The final and perhaps most important step in dropping shame and guilt is practicing self-empathy. Empathy can be described as the ability to understand and feel what the other person is feeling by putting yourself in their shoes. As we have seen so far, codependents are experts at recognizing and responding to the emotions of others. However, when it comes to their own feelings, they haven't a clue what they need.

Self-empathy is simply learning to treat yourself with the same kindness you treat others. Your friend can wrong you in the morning and by lunchtime, you are over it and back to being friends again. So why is it so easy to still feel ashamed or guilty for something you did ten years ago? The simple answer is that we do not show ourselves the same kindness we show to others.

When you lack self-empathy, you are overly critical of yourself. You bash yourself over every mistake and rarely take time to recognize your strengths. This self-negativity is common in codependents and it makes it easy for them to ignore their needs and focus on those of other people.

If you are always focusing on what is wrong with you and why you do not deserve any happiness you will spend your life in a cloud of guilt and shame. It is time to practice self-empathy. The first step in self-empathy is accepting your past and forgiving yourself.

There are many things you can do daily that will help you practice self-empathy.

Tips for self-empathy

1. Stop the negative self-dialogue

Why am I so stupid? Why can't he love me? I will never amount to anything. If you are the kind of person who has negative thoughts running on a continuous loop in your head, then congratulations! You are your own worst enemy.

Negative self-dialogue does more emotional and psychological damage than any external force can do. It becomes a self-fulfilling cycle where you become all those things you say about yourself.

So, if you are to free yourself from codependency, the first thing you need to do is stop the negative self-dialogue. This means that you have to be actively aware of what you are thinking throughout the day. When the negative thoughts start creeping up, immediately shift your focus to something else.

Curb the negative thoughts by interjecting with a positive. Something like, *maybe he left me but now I have more time to travel or spend with my family.* Always counter a negative thought with a positive. It will be difficult at first but slowly you will start to have more positive thoughts than negative ones.

Your thoughts become your reality. Changing negative self-talk is, therefore, a core step to changing your life and your outcomes.

2) Become more mindful

You would be surprised at just how much of our time is spent on auto-pilot mode. Becoming mindful means paying more attention to your thought, feelings, and needs. We have seen how negative self-dialogue can be damaging if you let it take root. Being mindful makes you more aware of what you are thinking and thus more control over your actions and behavior.

Mindfulness helps you step away from being reactive to being proactive. It helps you take responsibility for your actions and behavior since you stop simply reacting to what other people are doing and actively engage your own thoughts and emotions.

Mindfulness helps you live in the present and stop focusing on your past. It helps you treat emotions as passing events and not to over-identify with any one emotion.

Mindfulness practices like journaling, meditation and breathing exercises can help you get back to the present when you are feeling overwhelmed.

3) Spend time doing things that are important to you

Part of loving yourself is acknowledging your own needs and desires. Codependency may have made you put your needs aside to focus on pleasing others but its time to get back to loving yourself first. What do you enjoy? What are you passionate about? What would you do if you had more time?

These questions will help you identify the things you need more of in your life. The more you engage in things you are passionate about the less you will need to over-function in other people's lives. Spend time on your passions and desires. You will be much happier for it and your life will stop revolving around other people.

In the same vein stop doing things you hate just to please other people. This only makes you resentful and hurts your relationships in the end. Speak up and articulate what you do and do not like. You may have to compromise on some issues but at least you are no longer putting up just to get along.

Chapter 5: Freedom from Narcissism and Manipulation

Being in a relationship with a narcissist is like being in a room with a slow gas leak. You can smell the leak, you know something is wrong somewhere but you are not always sure where the stink is coming from. And just like in a gas leak, if you don't do something about it, the end result can be catastrophic.

In a normal situation, you would expect that leaving a toxic relationship would be easy after all you are miserable in it, so why is to so hard to leave? The more pertinent question is why is it so hard for a codependent to escape the narcissist's trap? Why is it so hard for them to leave these toxic situations even when they are desperately unhappy?

The simple answer is that narcissists are masters of covert manipulation. They have studied and identified your triggers. They know whether shame, guilt or blame are the buttons they need to push to get you to toe the line. They use this knowledge to not only manipulate you but hold you captive in an unhealthy relationship. They watch as you slowly but surely unravel bit by bit. That is the incredible hold of narcissism over codependents.

So how do you extricate yourself from these toxic relationships? How do you stop the cycle of emotional abuse and heal yourself? Well, first things first. You need to identify the warning signs that indicate you are being manipulated. Here are the most common ones.

1) Emotional blackmail

If you don't do this, I will kill myself, if you loved me you would...,
don't you want me to be happy? these are common phrases that
narcissists will use to manipulate you. If you dig deeper, you will
find that these types of phrases play to your feelings of fear, guilt
or shame.

This type of emotional blackmail is used by people who want to
control you. They use your own emotions against you and before
you know it, you are an enabler or a rescuer in constant service of
a narcissist.

If you are in a relationship where you are constantly being
emotionally blackmailed, it is time to wake up to the fact that you
are being manipulated by a narcissist.

2) The punisher

The punisher uses threats and sometimes actual harm to get you
to do what they want. Violent spouses fall neatly into this category.
They will "punish" you for disagreeing with them or not doing
something exactly the way they want it. They believe it is their role
to punish you because they know better than you.

This kind of narcissist is a control freak who wants obedience.
They have no interest in having an equal or healthy relationship.
They want to be your master and you the submissive subject.

Most people in relationships with this kind of narcissist
mistakenly think that the punisher will change. They are wrong.
This type of narcissist gets addicted to the power they feel when
abusing or inflicting pain on someone else.

A punisher will not get better and no matter what you do, they will always find something to punish you for. Your only option is to leave.

c) The sufferer

This type of narcissist is typically an addict of some kind. They use their misery and pain to guilt you into doing what they want. The sufferer uses fear and emotional blackmail to keep you in the dysfunctional relationships. They will say things like *if you leave me, I will die, or I cannot live without you, or you are my only hope.*

By doing this they are tapping into your need as a codependent to take care of other people's needs. You then get into a cycle of dependency that does not end. The more you help them, the needier they get and the more trapped you become.

Sufferers create a toxic dynamic where you feel responsible for their problems and are as a result, you are guilted into staying in a dysfunctional relationship.

The Path to Detachment

Once you identify the kind of manipulation that is being used to keep you in a dysfunctional situation. The next step is detachment. The important thing to remember is that manipulation is not just done by spouses. The narcissist in your life could be a parent, a child, a sibling or a friend. Codependent relationships are not just limited to marriage or love relationships.

Once you have identified the toxic relationship in your life. The first thing you want to do is detach from the codependency.

Detaching does not mean physically removing yourself from a situation or withdrawing from your responsibilities. In some cases, you will find that the person manipulating you is a child or a parent that you still need to maintain a relationship with.

You should, therefore, think of detaching not as breaking the relationship as a whole but as a means of breaking the codependency that exists in the relationship. What does this mean exactly? Detaching, in this case, means removing the emotional glue that is keeping you tied to a codependent situation.

Detaching means that you stop over-functioning in the other person's life and start focusing on your own needs. Physical closeness is often a non-factor for codependency. In fact, it is not uncommon to find separated couples who are codependent yet they live in separate homes. This means that when it comes to detaching while physical separation can help in some cases, it is not the main ingredient required for detaching successfully.

Detaching involves removing yourself from other's people's problems. It means that you take your emotions out of their situation and focus on your own life. What does that mean in real life? Let us say you are married to an alcoholic. So far you have been enabling them probably by providing the alcohol for them or giving them the means to acquire it.

Detaching means you completely stop doing those things. Simply stop getting involved in their addiction. If they want you to drive them to a store to pick up some beer, simply say no. It is no longer your responsibility to fuel their habit. You have to completely detangle yourself from their addiction.

It does not mean that you stop being concerned about the person. It just means that you can now use your concern in the right way by directing the person to seek help. When you are emotionally entangled in a situation you become incapable of making sound judgment calls. That is why detaching is a key step in breaking free from codependent relationships.

Detaching is focused on stopping the over-involvement. It makes it okay for you to empathize with someone without feeling the need to take on their burdens yourself.

Always remember that when you are trying to solve people's problems for them, you are denying them the opportunity to take responsibility for their own actions. No matter how good your intentions are, every time you get over-involved you are doing more harm than good.

Here are the key steps that are necessary for you to successfully detach from a codependent relationship.

1. Stop minimizing or hiding the problem

One of the key reasons we stay in relationships we have no business being in is a failure to accept reality. Stop basing your actions on what you wish would happen and start acknowledging the problem. Stop hoping your abusive partner will one day become prince charming if you love him just right. Stop telling yourself that the addict only needs one more hit and then they will stop.

The biggest trap that codependents fall into is denial. That is what keeps you in a dysfunctional situation. The first step in detaching is accepting reality. Look at the problem head-on and acknowledge the problem. Make admissions like: *this person is addicted and they need professional help* or *my husband is a narcissist and he will keep hitting me.*

Come to grips with the actual problem and then you can successfully detangle yourself from it.

2. Creating appropriate boundaries

Boundaries are crucial when it comes to detaching. They create a clear line that separates your responsibilities and needs from those of the other person. When you have clear boundaries, you will have a clear understanding that it is not your job to keep an addict happy by enabling them. You will understand that you are not responsible for keeping the narcissist's ego stroked.

Boundaries give you power because they create a clear distinction of where you stop and the other person begins. You cannot feel guilty about someone else's problems when you are clear that they are not your responsibility. Boundaries are what will tell you when you have done enough and the other person needs to pick up their own slack.

Boundaries will also allow you to focus on your own goals and needs. They will reduce your preoccupation with someone else's life and move your focus to your own life.

3. Live in the present

The third step in detaching is living in the present. What is your situation now? Forget the one nice thing your spouse did for you ten years ago that makes you feel beholden to him. How is he treating you now? Do not stay in a toxic situation because you are afraid you will be alone forever. Focus on the present. What is the best decision based on the current situation?

Living in the present frees you from guilt, shame, and blame. These three things keep you shackled to codependent relationships. That is why living in the present is an integral part of detaching.

The Power of No

For people-pleasers, there is hardly a word that is more difficult to say than the word no. If you have spent most of your life trying to get approval from others, then "no" is the exact antitheses of what you stand for. Yet there can be no escaping codependency without learning how to say no.

We often think of no as a negative word that is used to deny or forbid us from getting what we want. However, 'no' is one of the easiest ways to get your power back and assert your needs. Think of all the times you said yes when you really meant no. The more you agree to other people's demands and wishes the harder it gets to ever say no.

You, as a result, find yourself always playing along to get along no matter what you want. This is one of the reasons why codependent relationships always have underlying resentment behind them. When you are always saying yes to things you do not want, inevitably resentment starts to fester and you become angry about being made to do things you really do not want to do but agree to anyway.

When you have trouble saying no, you have a hard time being genuine or expressing your true feelings. You lose sight of what is important to you because you are working to keep other people happy. This is not only emotionally and physically draining but it can also make you miserable and unfulfilled in your relationships.

Narcissists know that codependents have a hard time saying no. They will ask you to do things you shouldn't be doing simply because they understand that you are a people pleaser. They will also use guilt, shame or blame to manipulate you into saying yes when you know the answer should be no.

How do addicts get their enablers to keep propping them up even when they know that it is wrong? They use manipulation and before the enabler knows it they are helping an addict stay addicted. If they had the ability and confidence to say no then the cycle of the codependency would effectively be broken.

'No' frees you from the obligation of people's expectations and needs. It gives you more time to focus on the things that you love and meeting your own needs. So how do you get better at saying 'no'? Here are some tips that will help.

i.   Be true to yourself. Don't shy away from voicing your true feelings and opinions.

ii.   Interrupt the yes cycle. If you are not comfortable saying 'no' outright, use an alternative deterrent like, *maybe next time*, or *I will get back to you on that* or something else along those lines. This way you can still turn someone down without hurting their feelings.

iii. Do not let guilt push you into saying yes when you mean no. Avoid getting emotional or overthinking your response.

iv.   Be simple and firm in your response. Do not try to justify or make excuses. A simple no will suffice.

Building Boundaries

Narcissists thrive in relationships where there are no boundaries. They walk all over your emotions and needs and have little respect for your opinion. That is why boundaries are a necessity if you are going to free yourself from a toxic codependent relationship with a narcissist.

Think of boundaries in the broader sense of the word. They let you know where the limits are. If you think of a country's boundaries for instance, they serve to tell people on the inside that you cannot cross beyond this point. People on the outside understand that you cannot just cross into someone else's space.

Emotional boundaries work in the same way. They safeguard what belongs to you and tell other people what lines they cannot cross. The boundaries you set up are the ones that set the pace for your relationship. If someone is treating you like a doormat, it is probably because you have not set up boundaries for your self and the relationship. This leaves you open to abuse and maltreatment.

Establishing boundaries starts with understanding your needs and choosing what you want from your relationship. Boundaries create the framework from which your relationship will operate. It, therefore, follows that you cannot have a healthy relationship without setting up healthy boundaries.

Here are the main ways in which you can establish healthy boundaries in your relationship.

1. Know your limits

The first step in building boundaries is off course identifying your limits. By this, we mean what behavior is acceptable and what is not. What are you willing to put up with and what is a deal-breaker? Use these parameters to draw a line that the other person is not allowed to cross.

For instance, you can say, *if you become aggressive, you can no longer live here.* This is a simple limit with a clear consequence that communicates your boundaries to the other person. If they choose to not respect it, then they know the consequence that will follow.

Do not feel the need to justify or explain your boundaries. Your limits should be based on what makes you comfortable and happy and not about pleasing the other person.

2. Be ready to enforce the consequence

Your limits will only work if you are willing to enforce the consequences of breaking them. You cannot keep letting someone cross the limit without enforcing the consequence and expect them to respect your boundaries.

For example, if you said *if you become aggressive, you can no longer live here,* then the person becomes aggressive and you do nothing about it, then your limits have no meaning.

Your boundaries are only as useful as your willingness to enforce them. If you are not willing to follow through on them, then your limits are just hollow words that will not deter the narcissist from manipulating you.

3. Keep the focus on yourself

The reason many people have a problem setting up limits and boundaries is that they are too focused on the other person's needs and feelings. Shift your focus back to your own wellbeing. Create limits that work for your needs and not ones that the other person will agree with or like.

You have to remember that people who love and care for you will not have a problem with you setting up healthy boundaries for yourself. If the other person is offended by your boundaries, then they probably did not care about you too much, to begin with.

Narcissists want you to remain open to abuse and manipulation so they will argue, threaten, attack and try to manipulate you. Be firm and stick to your limits. Boundaries are an essential part of any healthy relationship.

4. Have an exit plan

Be prepared to cut off contact with the narcissist. In some cases, the only way to get through to a narcissist is to cut off contact. If the manipulator is continuously pushing your limits, then it may be time to cut off contact.

Never put your happiness and well being in jeopardy to save a toxic relationship. Exiting a toxic relationship does not mean you failed, it simply means that you realize that you deserve better.

The Devil is In the Details

No matter how toxic a relationship is, leaving or detaching yourself from it is never easy. That is why the little things that you do in the process of detangling yourself will make a big difference in how you come out on the other side.

The last thing you want is to leave a relationship with so much emotional baggage that it affects your ability to have healthy and normal relationships in the future. Always know that the narcissist will resort to anything to keep you in the codependent relationship.

A narcissist will try to destroy your self-esteem so that you think they are the only person who will love you. They will make you feel like leaving them is the worst decision you can make. Keep in mind that their motives are selfish and the only reason they want you to stay is so that they have someone to walk all over.

Like we said at the beginning of the chapter, toxic relationships rarely get better. You have to muster the strength to walk away no matter how hard it is. The best way to do this is by learning to love yourself enough to want a better life for yourself. There is no reason you should resign yourself to an unhealthy relationship.

Here are simple ways to help you get past a bad relationship

i.   Do not keep reminders around you

Avoid having reminders or mementos of the person around you constantly. They only serve as painful reminders of the past. As much as possible keep reminders of past relationships to a minimum. Get rid of any pictures and gifts you may have and put them away somewhere you do not have to see them daily.

ii. Do not blame yourself

Some relationships work and some don't. Do not blame yourself or feel guilty about freeing yourself from a codependent relationship. Avoid negative thoughts or guilt about the failed relationship.

iii.   Surround yourself with love

This is a great time for you to spend time with family and friends. Staying close to family and friends helps you to overcome feelings of loneliness or isolation. Spending time with people you love will help you find your joy and you may actually find that you like the freedom of being free of the toxic relationship.

iv.   Do not jump into a new relationship

Give yourself time to heal after the relationship. Take time to reconnect with yourself. Jumping into a new relationship may take you back to the same toxic situation you worked so hard to escape. It is okay to be alone for some time as you learn to love and trust yourself again.

Chapter 6: Building Better Relationships

Now that you have broken free from your codependent relationship, what next? Relationships are an integral part of the human experience. We thrive on human connections and the ability to share our experiences with others. You, therefore, cannot self-isolate and swear off relationships just because you were in a dysfunctional relationship in the past.

As long as you have come to terms with your codependency and accepted your past, there is no reason there shouldn't be healthy and happy relationships in your future. Codependency is not a life sentence that should make you feel like you are incapable of having healthy connections with other people. You can still have meaningful relationships and make the best out of your life.

The key is to build better relationships that are based on mutual give and take. Once you have broken free from codependency you want to move to an interdependent relationship where you feel like an equal partner in a balanced equation.

In an interdependent relationship, both parties in the relationship are able to maintain their sense of self. This means that in contrast to a codependent situation, you are not looking for someone to validate or approve you. You already know who you are, you have your boundaries in place and you are ready to participate in the relationship as an equal partner.

If you are coming from a codependent relationship, you may have trouble recognizing what a healthy interdependent relationship looks like.

Here are the main characteristics of an interdependent relationship.

i. There is mutual love and respect in the relationship. You do not feel like you are the one who always has to give in or please the other party.

ii. Your needs are also important and both parties feel that they are emotionally engaged in the relationship.

iii. You have time to pursue and engage in personal interests

iv. You feel free to express your opinion and feelings without fear of being judged or blamed

v. You have healthy self-esteem and you are not constantly worrying what the other person thinks of you

vi. Both parties take responsibility for their own actions and behavior with no scapegoating or blame-shifting.

These are the qualities that lay the foundation for a healthy relationship. However, before you can build this kind of relationship, you need to first ensure that you are in the right place to become emotionally involved with someone else.

It Starts with Self Love; Building Self-esteem

A positive self-image is one of the prerequisites for building good relationships. It may be a cliché but expecting someone to love you if you cannot love yourself is a fallacy. Before getting into a relationship with someone else, the first thing is to ensure you have high self-esteem

Your self-esteem is primarily based on the opinion you have of yourself. It is no surprise that most codependent relationships involve a person with low self-esteem that is trying to get

88

validation from their partner. This means that they get into a relationship expecting the other person to make them feel better about themselves.

When you have a negative self-image, it becomes very hard to have a healthy relationship. You will try to cover up the parts of yourself that you think are flawed in order to please the other person. In so doing you hinder a true emotional connection from being created since you are not being genuine.

It is always strange how people can feel when we are not being genuine. Have you ever started dating someone and gotten this vibe that they are being fake or deceptive? This is because we have a natural instinct that enables us to sense what the other person is feeling. If you always come across like you are hiding something, then establishing a meaningful connection becomes difficult.

This is why healthy self-esteem is essential for a good relationship. It frees you up to be yourself and open to sharing and connecting with others. You do not need to hide or camouflage your feelings because you fully accept and love who you are.

The great thing about self-esteem is that it is something you can cultivate and build. If you have a negative self-image, you can gradually change that and become a confident and positive person.

Here are some easy ways to develop a positive self-image.

a) Stop with the negative self-talk

Sometimes we are our own biggest critics and this slowly undermines our self-esteem until it hits rock bottom. Be kind to yourself, stop finding fault with your appearance, performance or status in life. Learn to love who you are by appreciating your strengths.

Quash the negative thoughts and switch to a positive mindset. People treat us the way we teach them to treat us. If you are always putting yourself down, do not be surprised if others follow your lead and start doing it to you.

Train yourself to control your thoughts by being aware of what you are thinking. If negative thoughts start to catch hold counteract them with positive ones. Positive self-affirmation using mantras can help cancel out years of negative self-talk. Find a mantra that inspires you most and repeat it to yourself as often as you need to.

b) Stop comparing yourself with others

If you are always comparing yourself with others you are setting yourself up for disappointment. There is always someone better and someone worse off than you. Run your own race and focus on building yourself rather than checking your progress against others.

You do not have to be married by twenty-six just because your friend was or have a yacht because your old friend from college does. Everybody's journey is different. Learn to trust your journey and accept that your life is moving at the right pace for you.

c) Stop chasing perfection

If you are always holding yourself up to impossible standards then developing a negative self-image is par for the course. Being hard on yourself because you are not able to live up to unrealistic ideals or goals not only dents your self-esteem, it also makes it hard for you to accept yourself.

90

d) Focus on what you can change

Getting caught up in circumstances that you cannot change can leave you feeling helpless. Always focus on things that you can change. If you spend too much energy worrying about things beyond your control you hinder your ability to progress as a person. Your power lies in the things that you can change.

e) Spend time on the things that make you happy

Dedicate your time to hobbies and interests that keep you in a positive frame of mind. This is an effective way of avoiding negative self-talk. When you are having a good time, you tend to have a positive energy that helps to boost your confidence and self-esteem.

Once you start building your self-esteem you will find it easier to connect with people. This is because the positive self-image will give you the confidence to be yourself and to open up to other people.

As a plus, people who are confident tend to be more attractive to others. We all want to be around positive and happy people. Cultivating a positive self-image will naturally increase your draw on other people and encourage people to want to get to know you.

Ultimately, before you seek to build better relationships with others, first improve your relationship with yourself and learn to practice self-love.

Overcoming Jealousy and Anxiety in Relationships

Codependent relationships are characterized by feelings of anxiety and jealousy. It is therefore natural that when looking to build better relationships you would want to overcome the jealousy trap.

Jealousy can lead to overprotective behavior in a relationship. This behavior makes your partner feel smothered and stifled in the relationship. The net result of this is that the relationship gradually starts to break down and may eventually end due to the negative impact of jealousy.

Think of jealousy like a weed that slowly but surely starts to divert nutrients from the plant and in no time the starved plant withers and dies. That is the same effect that jealousy will have on your relationship.

Imagine how it feels to be in a relationship with someone who is constantly monitoring your every move. It creates a toxic environment in the relationship that chokes the life out of your emotional connection. No one wants to be constantly under a microscope in their relationship. For you to build a healthy relationship your partner needs to know you trust them.

Jealousy stems from our insecurities. Some are abandonment issues that we have had since childhood while others are insecurities that stem from having low self-esteem. Anxiety and jealousy in relationships can also be caused by a need to control others. Whatever the cause, jealousy, and anxiety are recipes for disaster in a relationship.

In most cases, jealousy and anxiety have more to do with your low self-esteem than with your partner's actions. This means that you have the power to control these emotions and prevent them from impacting your relationship negatively by working on your internal triggers.

Here are some effective strategies for overcoming jealousy and anxiety in your relationships.

1. Assess yourself

Jealousy is mostly a self-esteem issue that starts to project itself on others. You, therefore, need to first self-analyze to determine what is making you feel that way. the following questions can help you arrive at the root of your problem.

- ➢ Do I have a fear of abandonment?
- ➢ Do I often feel like my partner is too good for me?
- ➢ Am I always comparing myself with others?
- ➢ Do I feel like I cannot live without my partner?
- ➢ Has my partner given me any valid reason not to trust him?
- ➢ Do I spend too much time focusing on my partner?
- ➢ Do I have a life outside this relationship?

All these questions can help you determine whether your jealousy issue is internal or external. If most of your issues are internal, then you need to work on your self-esteem if you are to overcome your feelings of jealousy and anxiety.

Always remember that it is not your partner's responsibility to make you feel good about yourself. That is an inside job.

2. Manage your emotions

Feeling jealous is one thing, acting out, as a result of it, is a completely different thing. Once you recognize that you are feeling jealous. The next thing step you need to take is to manage your

93

emotions. Control the urge to lash out or have an emotional outburst. This will only make your partner more defensive and push them away from you.

Picture coming home to a partner who is always demanding to know where you were, who you were with and what you were doing? Not only is this kind of nagging tedious for both parties, but it also shows your partner that you do not trust him.

Unless your partner has given you a valid reason not to trust him, keep your feelings of jealousy and anxiety under control. Acknowledge your feelings but don't let them take control of your actions. Find a healthy outlet for your anxiety. You can use mindfulness practices such as meditation or yoga to center your emotions and avoid getting overwhelmed.

3. Seek your own sense of security

Jealousy, as we have seen, is often linked to a poor sense of self. When your happiness and self-worth are dependent on someone else, it is easy to become insecure. Insecurity then leads to feelings of jealousy and anxiety in your relationship. This is why it is important to develop your own sense of security.

Build a life for yourself that is separate from your relationship. Have your own interests and passions to keep you fulfilled and happy with your own life. When you start having a life that is not dependent on your partner, then you will be less prone to jealousy and insecurity.

Remember that any relationship has an equal chance of failing or succeeding. That means you cannot tie up all your self-worth in the relationship. There are so many other things in life that you can devote time to so that your life is well rounded.

Never let a relationship be your whole life, it should be a part of a wholesome life.

4. Express yourself

Never let feelings of jealousy or anxiety fester. They will only further dent your self-esteem and lead to unresolved anger issues. Confide in a friend, family member or even your partner and let them know how you are feeling. Talking to people helps to unburden yourself emotionally. You also get to see things from different perspectives that may help you understand your situation better.

5. Replace negative emotions with positive ones

Stop allowing negative thoughts to become dominant in your life. Make a conscious decision to focus on the positives in your relationship. If you feel yourself getting into a negative space, distract yourself. Get busy and look for things to keep your mind occupied.

Sometimes boredom may cause you to create imaginary problems that do not even exist. When you stay occupied, you are less likely to nitpick on your relationship. Stay positive and avoid letting jealousy take control of your life.

A simple trick is to use the rubber band technique. Simply place a rubber band on your wrist. Every time you feel the anxiety and jealousy start to invade your emotions snap the rubber band. This simple trick will help you consciously turn your thoughts away from the negative to more positive thoughts.

Building Freedom through Commitment

It may sound like a paradox but commitment is actually quite freeing. When you are in a healthy and stable relationship you are free to be yourself. You feel secure and safe enough to open up to the other person completely. Commitment comes with a sense of safety and security that stems from knowing that you have made a decision to be with someone.

Being unsure and perpetually searching breeds anxiety and fosters insecurity. That is why commitment can be such a freeing experience. For most people with codependency issues, commitment can be daunting. It stirs up old fears of abandonment and potential abuse. It is, therefore, no surprise that codependents often have trouble with commitment.

Of course, for commitment to work you first need to be sure of yourself, your values and what you want from the relationship. You cannot go into a commitment half-baked and expect it to work. Once you are in a place in your life when you are sure of yourself, your needs and your goals, you are then in a perfect position to enter into a commitment.

Commitments make us more efficient and focused because we have already chosen a path. Think of it this way, before you make a commitment you are not sure which direction you want to go in, your energy is all over the place and you are constantly searching for the right path.

Now fast-forward to the point at which you have already chosen the path to take. At this point, you are clear on where you are going and the anxiety has been taken out of the equation. At this point, all you need to do is focus on the path you have chosen to get to your destination. This is how commitment gives you freedom.

Commitment takes away the insecurity of the unknown and leaves you in a safe space where you are free to be yourself and be fully open to the other person. Once you realize that, you will have come a long way to overcoming your commitment issues.

How to overcome your commitment issues

1. Create freedom in your relationships

One of the biggest reasons people view commitment as a restriction on their life is the assumption that the other person takes control over your life. If this is your biggest commitment fear, you need to learn how to create space and freedom in your relationship.

You can do this by creating a relationship where each party is free to have their own interests and life outside the relationship. Commitment becomes an issue when one person feels stifled and limited. When you have enough space in your relationship for each person to still be an individual in their own right, then you will have discovered the freedom of commitment.

2. Be honest

Be brutally honest in your relationship so that the other person knows exactly what to expect and what is expected of them in the relationships. Many commitments become unsustainable because one or both parties enter into them with false expectations.

Share your feelings openly and also listen to the other person's point of view. This enables you to willingly enter into a commitment eyes-wide-open and avoid any feelings of deception down the line.

3. Tackle your emotions

If you have a fear of commitment, delving deep to find what triggers this fear may help you overcome it. You may find that you have a fear of abandonment and thus choose to stay safe by detaching yourself. You may have reservations about your partner which are holding you back or you may even be unsure of your own intentions.

Whatever the trigger for your fear of commitment is, once you are aware of it then you are better placed to deal with it. Do not just be reactive in nature, build your emotional aptitude by taking time to find the triggers behind your emotions. You may find that your fear of commitment is buried deep in your past and actually has nothing to do with the present or your relationship.

How to Not Lose Yourself in a Relationship

A relationship is made up of two individuals. Not a person and a half, or a person who is an extension of another. Losing yourself in a relationship is a common mistake that people especially those with codependent tendencies tend to make.

Retaining your sense of self and identity is an important part of a healthy relationship. No matter how much you love someone, you should never forget who you are, your values, interests, and personal goals.

If you are prone to accommodating, compromising, justifying and fawning, then you are susceptible to losing yourself in relationships. These are classic traits that codependents are prone to that make them sacrifice their own needs for the sake of their relationships.

Here are some tips to help you retain your identity and self-worth in your relationship.

1.Know who you are. Hold on to your values, interests and personal goals even when you are in a relationship. Have a well-developed sense of who you are and what you want out of life in general.

2. Be assertive. Always articulate your needs and feelings in your relationship. A relationship is built on mutual give and take. Do not take on the role of a giver and forget your own needs.

3. Have strong boundaries. Set clear limits and boundaries in your relationship. This will help you stay true to yourself and avoid compromising your identity.

4. Have your own friends. Do not be the kind of person who ditches their friends when they get into a relationship. Always make time for friends and family when you are in a relationship.

5. Stop over-functioning in the other person's life. Know the difference between your responsibilities and the other person's responsibilities. Do not take on the other person's roles and neglect your own needs. A healthy relationship is made up of two equal partners that are each responsible for their own actions.

6. Have your own life. A relationship does not mean giving up your interests, passions or career. Pursue your goals and passions and create a well-rounded life for yourself. Never let a relationship be the only thing you have going for you.

Chapter 7: Emotional Intelligence

> *Until you make the unconscious conscious, it*
> *will direct your life and you will call it fate.*
> C J Jung

Intelligence is a concept we often associate with our cognitive aptitude and concepts like book smarts. However, did you know that research has found that being emotionally intelligent is actually a more accurate determinant of success on both personal and professional levels?

Emotional intelligence has been found to equip people with personal and social competencies that enable them to function better in personal and professional relationships. This means that emotional intelligence is a vital component for better relationships.

Being emotionally intelligent can be defined as having the ability to recognize and manage your own emotions and those of others. It comprises of four key skills namely: self-awareness, self-regulation, social awareness, and relationship management.

The combination of these four skills gives you personal and social competencies. These competencies enable you to have control of your own emotions and a deeper understanding of yourself. They also enable you to have an understanding of other people that enables you to relate better with them.

The first thing you need to understand about emotions is that there is no escaping them. Even the most stoic amongst us are still susceptible to emotions since they are a natural part of the human experience. In fact, our emotional brain, the limbic system, is always the first point at which the brain interprets external messages and stimuli.

This means that even before you have had time to consider a situation rationally, the limbic system in your brain has already processed it on an emotional level. Therefore before you think anything, you first feel it. That in itself makes emotions a powerful driving force in our behavior and actions.

As a codependent person, you probably experience a roller coaster of emotions on a day to day basis. This is due to the fact that you act as a sponge, constantly soaking up other people's emotions. This lack of boundaries between your emotions and those of others makes it hard for you to self regulate.

If for instance, you depend on other people to feel happy, then you have no control over your emotions since you are simply reacting to other people's emotions. This creates an unhealthy dependence on others that promotes the development of codependent tendencies. Since codependents have poor boundaries, developing emotional intelligence is the only way to overcome the emotional turmoil that can take over their lives.

Apart from enabling you to self regulate and manage your own emotions, emotional intelligence also helps you to understand other people's emotions. This is key to forming healthy relationships with others. When you can recognize and understand your partner's emotions it allows you to connect with them on a deeper level.

How does emotional intelligence make your life better?

i. It makes you more adaptable and open to change. Emotionally intelligent people find it easy to accept change and adapt to new situations.

ii. It increases your empathy for others and enables you to see things from their perspective.

iii. It gives you more control over your emotions and therefore more power over your actions and behavior.

iv. It makes you better at resolving conflicts and managing relationships.

v. It helps you learn to accept criticism without letting it affect your self-esteem.

vi. It increases your emotional availability.

vii. It decreases your codependence on other people

While most of our emotional intelligence skills develop early in life during our childhood years, this is still a skill that you can successfully cultivate in yourself. If you are tired of feeling like a prisoner to your emotions, it is time to start working on your emotional intelligence skills.

People who want to have better relationships also need to cultivate emotional intelligence. A keen understanding of other people's emotions is necessary if you are to build and manage your relationships effectively.

So where do you begin to if you want to become emotionally savvy? Here are some effective tools that will help you increase your emotional intelligence.

1. Realize that sometimes being good is better than being right

Many relationships have been broken down by one person's need to be right all the time. Part of being emotionally intelligent is being aware of your partner's feelings and understanding them. This awareness should help you realize that you do not always have to be right.

If you have a penchant for trying to win every argument, you may be winning the battle to lose the war. Winning an argument may feel good at the moment but is it really worth damaging your relationship for? A big part of being emotionally intelligent is knowing how to pick your battles.

Do not always be hell-bent on proving yourself right at the cost of the other person's feelings. You will only end up alienating people and make them less likely to open up to you. Always have the bigger picture in mind.

2. Sit with your feelings

If you have heard it once, you have probably heard it a hundred times; *do not make decisions when you are mad*. We all know this to be true, yet we often make decisions in the heat of the moment only to regret our actions later.

Sit with your emotions for a while. Hold back the nasty retort and find a healthy outlet for your feelings. Emotions cloud your judgment and make you reactive in nature. Reactive behavior gives your power away to the other person since you start to act and behave based on your emotional reaction.

Count to five, walk away or simply distract yourself if you feel you are about to lose it. You can revisit the situation once you feel calm enough to keep your feelings in check.

3. Question your opinions

It is good to have opinions and perspectives on various things but do not always assume your opinion is the only opinion. Learn to question your opinion and adapt to new situations. Question your values and beliefs regularly. You will be surprised how much you can learn when you decide to be open-minded.

If people never questioned their opinions, we would still be stuck on the assumption that the earth is flat.

4. Learn to take criticism

A fragile ego can be your greatest weakness when it comes to cultivating emotional intelligence. If you are one of those people who simply cannot take criticism, you may be letting your emotions get the better of you. Criticism may not always be right or called for, but knowing how to take it in stride will help you have healthier relationships.

You do not have to agree with a criticism to take it in good grace and move on from it. Build enough self-esteem that criticism does not feel like a personal attack on you. At best criticism can help you improve and become better. Even when it is not constructive, criticism still allows you to understand what the other person is thinking.

5. Know your triggers

Self-awareness is a major facet of emotional intelligence. Always know your triggers and the situations that cause you to lose control of your emotions. If for instance, you know that trust is a big issue for you, getting involved with a deceitful person hoping they will change is a recipe for disaster.

When you know your triggers, it means that you know your limits. This enables you to pick situations that you need to avoid and those that will be good for you.

6. Learn to recognize other people's emotions

Do not be the person in the room who does not pay attention to anyone else but expects everyone else to listen to them. Social awareness is a big part of emotional intelligence. It involves being able to read other people's emotions and opinions from verbal and non-verbal cues.

Strive to hear what the other person is trying to communicate. This will give you a better understanding of their emotions and from this, you will know the best way to respond to them.

You should be able to tell when what you are saying or doing is making the other person uncomfortable. This ability to read other people's emotions will go a long way in helping you build better relationships. If you are always caught up in your own needs and feelings, you cannot figure out the best way to connect to people.

Learn to appreciate feelings beyond your own and be sensitive to other people's needs.

7. Find stress-relieving techniques

We are most vulnerable to our emotions when we are stressed. Stress management techniques can help to make you feel centered and give you better control over your emotions. There are plenty of de-stressing techniques such as meditation, yoga or breathing exercises.

For some people even just communing with nature on a walk is enough to relieve anxiety and stress. Others find music soothing while for some physical exercise is the best stress buster. Find a method that works for you and make it part of your regular schedule.

The Hand You're Dealt

Most of our personality traits are carried from childhood. This is because the brain grows most in our formative years before the age of eight. That means that the connections that brain cells make in childhood remain with us all the way into adulthood and determine the personality traits we develop.

As we discussed in the first three chapters, most of the codependency tendencies you exhibit can be traced back to childhood experiences. Children who had to live with dysfunction will often develop codependency as a coping mechanism to help them deal with their environment. Unfortunately even after you are no longer in the dysfunctional situation, the codependent traits remain part of your personality.

So how do you get past the hand that fate dealt you? After all, you did not choose what kind of situation you were born into so shouldn't you be free to break the hold your past has on your emotions and personality traits? Like everything else permanent change takes time and a willingness to confront your past.

Most codependents who were scarred by their childhood will bury the unpleasant experiences in an attempt to forget them. Unfortunately, all this does is leave you with unresolved issues. To be free of your past, you must be willing to acknowledge it and the role it has played in your life. Only then will you be able to really let it go and move on with your life.

Do not be afraid to seek help in the form of therapy or support groups to help you deal with codependency tendencies that are tied to your past. Therapy gives you a safe space to confront your inner demons and resolve them. It may not work overnight, but you will find that facing your past will slowly start to unburden you off emotional baggage that you have carried with you for yours.

Ultimately, you can choose to not leave your outcomes up to fate by denying your past power over your future. Start by building your self-awareness using the techniques we have discussed. Once you have identified where your codependency issues stem from, the next step is to seek help and start your journey to recovery.

EFT Therapy Techniques; Restore Broken Relationships

Codependent relationships typically cause a lot of emotional and psychological damage. Whether you are an enabler, caretaker, a rescuer or any other type of codependent, you will find that the effect of codependency leaves a lot of emotional damage in its wake.

Recovering from codependency is one thing but you also need to heal and repair your broken relationships. This is because not every codependent relationship ends with you cutting off the other person from your life completely. This means that you need to find a way to restore the broken relationship to a functional and healthy level. One of the most effective ways to do this is by using EFT therapy.

EFT refers to emotionally focused therapy. It is only natural that one of the most effective therapies for healing codependent relationships targets your emotional health. This is because emotions are the driving forces behind most relationships.

EFT therapy techniques focus on resolving issues in unhealthy relationships and restoring broken relationships. EFT is designed to help improve the nature of emotional attachment and connection in relationships. It is intended as a means through which the bonding and attachment processes that make up our relationships can be repaired and restored.

By using EFT therapy, couples are able to recognize their emotional responses as well as those of their partners. This helps them to not only identify the patterns that cause a relationship to break down but it also builds intimacy and fosters strong bonds. The aim of this process is to help re-establish the emotional connection in relationships that had broken down.

EFT therapy uses a combination of the principles of attachment theory and person-centric therapy. It fosters reconciliation and mending of relationships by helping the two parties in a broken relationship to understand the role of their emotional reactions in the health of the relationship.

In EFT therapy, the main premise is that most problems that arise in relationships are due to codependency fears such as the fear of abandonment. This type of fear hinders an individual's ability to form healthy attachments to other people. The person then becomes emotionally unavailable which only leads to a breakdown in the relationship.

By restoring the ability of couples to meet each other's emotional needs, EFT therapy helps to foster healthy attachment between two people and mend broken unions. EFT therapy covers a wide range of issues that are common causes of conflict in relationships and teaches couples how to de-escalate conflict, address deeper feelings and uncover underlying issues that may lead to codependent tendencies.

Emotionally Focussed Therapy occurs in different stages that are designed to address the emotional distress in relationships.

These are the key stages involved in EFT therapy.

1. De-escalation.

This step is intended to help couples identify the key areas of conflict in their relationship. It involves figuring out how negative emotions interfere with conflict resolution and hinder you from solving the issue amicably.

In this stage, the therapist will highlight your underlying issues and help you to see how reframing the conflict and looking at it from a different perspective can help to resolve it.

2. Altering interaction patterns

From de-escalation, EFT therapy moves on to altering or changing negative patterns of interaction between the two people in a relationship. Most relationships will breakdown due to negative interaction patterns such as blaming, shaming or controlling behavior.

Once a couple is able to successfully change from negative interactions to healthier ways of bonding, they have a better chance of restoring a broken relationship. In this stage, EFT focuses on teaching the partners to recognize and be mindful of each other's needs and emotions.

3. Consolidation and integration

The final stage of emotionally focused therapy revolves around developing new communication skills and interaction patterns. This is aimed at building healthy modes of interaction through open and honest communication.

The aim here is for the couple to change from old and dysfunctional ways of communication to healthier interaction patterns. Once these changes are successfully implemented, the broken-down relationship has a chance of becoming a healthy relationship that is free of codependency.

The Gift of Goodbye

Letting go is never easy. We like the comfort of the familiar and love to love what we have always known. However, sometimes goodbye is the best gift you can give yourself. The gift of goodbye is giving yourself permission to walk away from things that keep dragging you back and slowing down your progress.

A simple analogy that is used to elaborate on the importance of letting go is that of a boy who is trying to get some candy from his father. His arms are outstretched but he cannot take the candy because there is something else already in his palm. His father tells him, that if he wants the candy, the only way to get it is to empty his palms first.

At first, the boy is reluctant because he wants both what is already in his hand and the candy his father is offering him. Eventually, he comes to the realization that his hands can only hold so much so he has to choose one or the other. He drops whatever he was holding and his father places the candy in his now empty palm.

This simple illustration just goes to show that we can only hold so much in terms of emotions within us. At some point, you have to spring clean and make room for better experiences. Yes, it may be scary but if you are unwilling to let go of the past you will never be ready for a new future.

If you are healing from codependency, there are plenty of old hurts and scars that got you where you were. Now that you have chosen the path to recovery, it is time to release your past and make room for the future. Sad as it may be, some relationships cannot be healed and the only way to move on from them is to have the courage to let them go.

Goodbye is not just about saying goodbye to relationships, it involves letting go of habits that drag you down, toxic values and self-destructive beliefs. At this point in the book, you have already self-analyzed and identified the toxic bits in your life and the strengths that will take you forward.

Shed the toxicity and the emotional baggage and prepare for a better future that is not bogged down by your past. Letting go is a gradual process, it is not something you can do overnight. However once you have made the first step, the rest will be easier and you will find it easy to embrace the positive change in your life.

Effective strategies for letting go of emotional baggage

1. Identify your unresolved issues

This may be uncomfortable but be brutally honest with yourself. In most cases you will find that you already know what your main issues are, we just find it easy to camouflage or deny that they exist. List them all in order from the most prevalent followed by the not so major ones.

These could be things that happened in the past, like bullying in school or things that are happening in the present like being overweight or a bad relationship. Whatever the issue is, pick something that you realize your life would be better without.

List them down clearly in one column.

2. Who is to blame?

Look at the issues you have listed. Who is responsible for each of them. Do you blame yourself, a parent, your spouse? Whoever it is, mark the name next to the issue connected to that person. If you blame yourself, that's also okay, put your name down for the issues you feel you are responsible for.

3. What is the consequence?

You now have an unresolved issue and the responsible party, the next step is to answer what has the unresolved issue done to your life. Do you have low self-esteem, as a result, have you had bad relationships, as a result, are you chronically stressed?

Whatever the answer is, note it down next to the issue so that you can clearly see the unresolved issue, the responsible party and the consequence it has hard on your life.

4. What opportunity are you missing out on?

What impact has the unresolved issue had on your life? Did you lose a job? Do you have a hard time having meaningful relationships? Whatever the unresolved issue has cost you, note it down. It could be one or multiple opportunities.

5. The fix

Now that you have a clear path from what the issue is and what it is costing you, what can you do to fix it? Does it involve forgiving the person and mending the relationship? Do you need to forgive yourself and let go of the past? Do you need to walk away from a toxic relationship?

At this point the solution should be clear, all you need is the courage to make the decision.

Chapter 8: Healing Pleasures

When you have spent most of your life caring for other people, looking after their needs and pretty much loving everyone but yourself, getting back to self-love is not always easy. Changing from an externally focused person to caring for your own needs is an essential part of your healing process.

The best way to focus inward is to spend some time alone. This will allow you to focus on meeting your own needs without worrying about other people. Whether this means taking a holiday or putting some distance between you and your daily life, do whatever it takes to get some time to reconnect with yourself.

If you have embarked on a new relationship, allow yourself to be loved. It may be strange having someone meet your needs for the first time but you need to get used to what it means to be in a healthy and balanced relationship. Avoid falling back into old codependent patterns. Always be self-aware and look out for warning signs that you may be falling back to old patterns of behavior.

In your recovery process, do not forget to have fun. Making happy memories can help you get past your old hurts. New happy memories can replace the old sad ones and help you to emerge stronger and more secure in yourself. This is the time to rediscover your interests and develop new passions that will allow you to get to know yourself better and have fun as you do it.

When you rediscover what your goals, interests, and passions are. You can plan activities around these three areas that will help you in becoming the best possible version of yourself. Remember your goal at this point is not just to ditch the old codependency tendencies, but to create new healthy habits that will keep you occupied on the road to bettering your life.

One of the challenges you may face is learning to trust and love again. Once we have been through a damaging relationship it is natural to want to protect ourselves by avoiding intimacy and relationships. Do not deny yourself a chance at happiness because you are afraid that history may repeat itself.

Spend as much time alone as you need to feel whole again but do not give up on love and relationships. Ultimately, relationships make our lives much richer. Sharing your experiences with someone who loves and cares for you is a natural part of a healthy life. Always be open to the possibility of love and trust that you have moved on from codependency.

Overcoming the Fear of Intimacy

We have already looked at some of the fears that may predispose you to become codependent. These are fears like the fear of abandonment, the fear of rejection and other insecurities. These unresolved issues make it difficult to open up to others and form deep connections with them.

If you are on the road to recovery from codependency, it is possible that these fears will still plague you. This means that you have to find a way to overcome them if you are to have truly open and meaningful connections with people. As long as you remain emotionally unavailable, your relationships will continue to be dysfunctional.

Emotional intimacy goes beyond the physical aspects of your relationships. It is possible to have a physical relationship with someone without being emotionally intimate with them. Emotional intimacy requires complete openness on an emotional level and the willingness to bare your innermost feelings to the other person.

This kind of intimacy breeds a sense of security and safety in knowing that you can be completely true to yourself without needing to suppress or camouflage your emotions. Getting to this point in a relationship is never easy, and it can be especially hard for codependents who have a history of dysfunction and abuse in their relationships.

So how do you get over your fear of intimacy? Is it possible to get past unresolved abandonment issues and trust people enough to let them into your life?

Here are some effective strategies that will help you get past your fear of intimacy.

1. Identify your triggers

In most cases, your fear of intimacy will be due to unresolved issues from your past. Self-analyzing and identifying what triggers your fear of intimacy will help you address it objectively. Were you neglected as a child? Did you have a bad relationship that made it difficult to trust other people?

Whatever your trigger is, it is important to realize that unresolved issues only leave you with emotional baggage that affects the health of your potential relationships. Whether it will take some therapy, self-forgiveness or forgiving others to get past your fears, do not ignore your unresolved issues.

Identifying your triggers is the first step to releasing them. As difficult as it is, facing your unresolved issues is one of the best ways to unburden yourself. Take the first step to dumping your emotional baggage by seeking help for your unresolved issues.

2) Be your own best friend

This is as opposed to constantly criticizing and finding fault in yourself and your actions. The fear of intimacy can be enhanced by low self-esteem that makes you feel unworthy of love. This negative self-image makes you avoid getting emotionally involved to minimize the chance of rejection.

Stop criticizing yourself constantly. Focus on your strengths and accept your flaws. No one is perfect and always talking yourself down does nothing but dent your confidence. Every day look in the mirror and find something you like about yourself.

Never allow negative thoughts to dominate your mind. You have the power to create a positive self-image but this will only happen if you learn to be kind to yourself. The more self-confident you feel about yourself, the less the fear of rejection that you will experience. This will make it easier for you to open up and take a chance on intimacy.

3. Find a way to de-stress

Stress tends to amplify our anxiety and minimize our self-confidence. Finding an effective way to manage negative emotions such as stress will help you develop a positive outlook.

Yoga, mediation and exercise are simple ways to not only boost your confidence but also minimize the stress levels in your life. The happier you are, the more open you will be to intimacy.

Taking care of your body also helps to boost your confidence and self-esteem levels which again makes a big difference in how you view intimacy.

4. Do you know what you want?

Sometimes our fear of intimacy has more to do with the person we are in a relationship with than with our unresolved issues. If you are not sure the person is right for you, then do not rush into intimacy. Intimacy makes any connection deeper and more meaningful but it will only work if you are with the right person.

Figure out what you want out of the relationship. This will give you the confidence to either become intimate or hold off on it until you are sure of your motives and goals. Indecision can be just as damaging as making the wrong choice so always make a point to identify what you want from a relationship early on.

5. Practice being vulnerable

Just as you cannot fish from the shore, you cannot overcome your fear of intimacy by avoiding relationships. Put yourself out there and take a chance that you can handle any outcome in your relationship. Start small by initiating contact with someone you like even if it is just as a friend. The more you do this, the better you will get at letting yourself be vulnerable.

If you are not ready for an intimate relationship. Take small baby steps that will slowly help you get past your fear of intimacy. Start by opening up to close friends and family and get used to being

119

vulnerable and exposed. This way when it is time for an intimate relationship it will not be as daunting or scary.

Disrupting Self-Defeating Values

Self-defeating behavior is common not just in codependents but in other personality types as well. Self-defeating beliefs or values are a set of traits that reflect pervasive and inflexible traits that we have developed over time. Most of these self-defeating values are developed as self-defense or coping mechanisms to help us deal with our environment and various situations.

Self-defeating values impact your self-confidence and hinder your ability to have healthy relationships. They put you in a continuous cycle of repeating patterns that become the order of the day in your life. You start to realize that your life is unfolding in predictable patterns.

The danger of self-defeating values is that they box you into a little corner and minimize your options and opportunities. For instance, if one of your self-defeating beliefs is love addiction, then you will always operate based on a belief that your life only means something when you are in a relationship. This means you will be incapable of conceiving of happiness outside of a relationship.

Self-defeating values are akin to putting a straight jacket on yourself that limits your range of thoughts, emotions, and beliefs.

Here are some of the most common self-defeating values that may be impacting your life.

1. **Perfectionism**. This may seem like a noble idea but since perfection is not possible it only makes you feel bad about yourself.

When you are constantly falling short of your unrealistic expectations your self-esteem is shattered.

2. **Achievement addiction** is similar to perfectionism. If you have this belief, you have attached your sense of self-worth to achieving certain milestones such as career, income, looks and so on. Again, this limits your ability to appreciate small victories in your life and sets you up for constant disappointment.

3. **Approval addiction** is another self-defeating value that predisposes you to codependency. If you have this belief you get your validation from pleasing and getting acceptance from other people. This is likely to make you over function in other people's lives, which is a classic symptom of codependent tendencies.

4. **Blaming**. This self-defeating belief breeds the inability to accept responsibility for your own mistakes. In this case, you hold other people accountable for your happiness, your actions, and your mistakes. If you have this belief you may be manipulative and prone to narcissistic behavior.

5. **Self-guilt**. This is the opposite of blaming and is a common self-defeating belief in codependents. It allows them to take on other people's problems and take on roles like the enabler and the caretaker.

The problem with self-defeating beliefs is that they can impede our growth by narrowing down our thinking. Our thoughts ultimately become our reality and your world will only stretch as far as your mind allows it to. If your life is bogged down by self-defeating values, you will find that your life is restricted to a few self-repeating patterns.

Unless you change your beliefs, it will be almost impossible to escape the destructive patterns in your life. You therefore first need to identify the limitations you have placed in your life with self-defeating beliefs and then actively start to change those beliefs.

The danger of self-limiting beliefs is that they lead to generalizations. This is where you paint all situations in your life with a broad brush and then respond with the pre-programmed response you have trained yourself to use. This not only limits your opportunities but also denies you the chance to have new experiences and have better outcomes.

Tips for overcoming self-defeating values

1. Identify your self-defeating beliefs

Recognize the self-limiting beliefs that have taken hold in your life. Do you often put off important tasks because you are afraid of failing? Do you always try to please other people because you need them to approve and validate you? Are you always chasing relationships because you are afraid of being alone?

Your self-limiting beliefs will always manifest in your actions so if you look closely at your behavior you will identify the self-defeating behavior behind it. Whether you are always procrastinating, people-pleasing or chasing perfection, these tendencies all result from self-defeating values that you have created in your mind.

2. Understand the emotion that triggers the behavior

Once you have identified your self-defeating values. You can now look for the emotions that trigger these tendencies. For instance, is your procrastination caused by performance anxiety, is your codependence driven by the fear of rejection? Behind every self - defeating behavior you will find that there is an emotion driving it.

That emotion is what you need to deal with in order to break the cycle. As long as the emotion remains, you will keep engaging in self-defeating behavior because you use it as a coping mechanism to deal with the negative emotion.

If you learn to manage your emotions you will find it easier to break the self-defeating patterns of behavior. You can use any of the emotional intelligence techniques we highlighted in chapter seven to improve your level of self-regulation.

3. Change the negative self-dialogue

The thoughts you have running constantly in your head have a bigger impact on your emotions than you realize. These negative thoughts may be pushing you to self-defeating behavior such as people-pleasing and seeking approval from others.

Take charge of your thoughts by being mindful and self-aware. Make a conscious effort to stem negative thoughts. Use positive mantras and affirmations to boost your self-esteem and cancel out negative thoughts.

4. Develop Self-Supporting Behaviors

The easiest way to break a habit is to replace it with a new one. So, start developing self-supporting behavior that negates or goes counter to your self-defeating values. For instance, if you are always trying to please other people, shift your focus to doing things that make you happy.

Every time you are faced with a choice pick the option that negates any of the self -defeating values you identified. Slowly but surely you will start to break the cycle and create new behavior patterns.

The only thing that is required for change to take hold is consistency. This means you should keep practicing the new behavior until it becomes second nature.

Cultivating Mindfulness

Mindfulness is being consciously present in the moment. At any given moment in time, there is a myriad of thoughts running through your mind. Thoughts of the past and plans for the future run on a continuous loop in your mind until there is little space left for what is going on in the present moment.

When you are mindful, you make a conscious effort to focus all your attention on the present. This means that you are not worrying about what happened last week or last year or planning what you need to be doing tomorrow. You are simply existing in the present moment and focussing your attention and awareness on what is happening at that point in time.

Mindfulness stems from being consciously in control of what your thoughts are and what you choose to focus on. Mindful living occurs when you consciously choose to take part in your life and build your awareness of the present and dissociate from mental experiences.

Much of our stress and anxiety stems from our concerns for the future or emotions triggered by experiences from our past. This is why mindfulness is one of the most effective stress management techniques. It brings your focus away from negative thoughts and emotions and allows you to focus on the present and revel in the moment.

Have you ever looked back at a situation and realized that you spent so much time worrying about it and that the worrying was much worse than the situation itself? Preoccupation robs you of your time and denies you the opportunity to enjoy the little pleasures of life.

In the east, Buddhists have long used mindfulness and meditation as a technique to center themselves and release negative energy. When we operate on autopilot, we have no control over what we are thinking or feeling, we are simply going through the motions and letting our minds roam free. To be truly mindful involves the following principles;

- Being fully aware of yourself, others and your surroundings.

- Intentional focusing and observing.

- Describing situations and experiences with words.

- Choosing to not focus on thoughts and feelings of the past or future

- Being impartial to mental experiences.

Simple techniques for cultivating mindfulness

1. Mindful breathing

Mindful breathing does not require you to be sitting in a meditative pose for you to practice it. You can use this technique anywhere whenever you are feeling stressed, overwhelmed or angry.

Simply focus inward and start taking deep breaths. Inhale to a count of 6, hold your breath for 2 seconds, then a long exhale. Repeat this deep breathing technique for about three minutes or until you start to feel calm and serene.

It will only take a few minutes of deep breathing to regain a sense of calm and bring your awareness back from your thoughts and feelings to the present moment.

2. Yoga

Yoga is a combination of physical, mental and spiritual exercises that incorporates breathing techniques, body movement, and meditation. The main aim of yoga exercises is to create a sense of emotional and mental balance. Yoga will help you achieve a mindful state by;

✓ Increasing your levels of self-awareness and self-control
✓ Increasing your ability to manage anxiety and stress.
✓ Improving mental clarity.

3. Mindful meditation

In mindful meditation, the goal is usually to focus your mind on the thoughts, sensations, and emotions that you are experiencing in the present or current moment. It generally involves control of breathing, muscle and body relaxation, mental imagery and a keen awareness of the body and mind.

There are many benefits of meditation including:

✓ Increased self-awareness.

126

✓ Improved attentiveness and mental clarity.
✓ Better self- regulation and management of emotions.
✓ Significant reduction of stress and anxiety levels.

Simple Ways to Love Yourself Everyday

Making yourself a priority is not always easy. We often find ourselves caught up in caring for others and meeting their needs. It can, therefore, be difficult to go from being focused on other people's happiness to ensuring your own. To make the process easier, instead of thinking of self-love as one big process, think of it as a series of small steps that you can take on a daily basis.

Knowing what makes you happy is an integral part of being a whole person capable of loving themselves and others. That's why when we looked at self-awareness, we highlighted the need to find out what your passions and interests are. Simply doing more of the things you love is one way of loving yourself.

Here are simple things you can do every day to love yourself.

1. Find something to compliment yourself about every day

It may be as simple as appreciating your cooking skills when you make a delicious meal, or how well you handled a conflict at work. Whatever it is, you can always find good things about yourself if you look.

Think of how quick we are to commend our friends for their accomplishments and good deeds. You also need to be your own cheerleader and recognize when you have done something good for yourself or others.

Learn to appreciate yourself, it is good for your confidence. It will also motivate you to do even better.

2. Embrace who you are

Self-love means seeing your flaws and loving yourself anyway. Give up on chasing perfection or anybody else's idea of who you need to be. Every day, look at your life and accept it. You may not be perfect but you are a work in progress and tomorrow will be better.

3. Do something that makes you happy every day

Do not get so caught up in life that you forget to carve out time for the things you love. Make a conscious decision to schedule time every day to do something you love. It could be reading a book by your favorite author, going for a walk or simply sitting in a quiet room for a while. Whatever it is that does it for you, make time for it.

4. Avoid toxic people

Let's face it, misery loves company and if you surround yourself with negative Nancy's do not be surprised if you are always miserable. Pick your friends wisely and avoid energy vampires who suck all the positive energy out of your life.

Focus on creating fewer but deeper connections as opposed to having a large group of friends that you do not even particularly like. When it comes to friendships, quality not quantity is the key.

5. Try something new

There is no better confidence boost that venturing out of your comfort zone and doing something new. Challenge yourself every day to do at least one thing you would not normally do. At the very least you may learn something new about yourself in the process.

6. Live in the moment

Focus on your present. Your life is happening now and every moment you spend worrying about the past or fretting about tomorrow is a moment you will never get back.

7. Stop overthinking everything

Add a bit of spontaneity in your life by going with the flow every once in a while. Not everything has to be perfect or well planned out all the time. Let your hair down every once in a while, and enjoy the moment. If you take life too seriously you may miss out on all the beautiful moments.

Chapter 9: Rewrite Your Story

Change is scary. The fear of the unknown and the comfort of the familiar are just some of the reasons we remain stuck in certain stages of our life. Often you will know that you need to make a change but the fear of the unknown keeps you paralyzed and unable to move.

This reluctance to embrace change can leave you stuck in a bad situation for years. Sadly, time waits for no one and the more you stay in limbo the more that life passes you by. Part of the reason that keeps us from changing our lives is that we are always waiting for just the right moment.

You want all your ducks to line up neatly in a row before you take your shot. This of course never happens and ten years later you are still living the same life, having the same struggles and still waiting for just the right moment to make your move.

Indecision, procrastination and the fear of the unknown have been the downfall of many dreams for a better life. You know what you need to do, you may even know how you need to do it, but still, you hang on to the safety of the status quo. Unless you can find the will and the strength to implement changes in your life, you will remain stuck in your cycle of codependency for a long time.

Rewriting your story simply means that you stop waiting for things to happen and start making things happen. The difference between the two is that in one scenario, you are in a reactive role, waiting for life to throw things at you so you can respond accordingly. In the second role, you are the one making things happen and life is responding to you. That is the fundamental difference between a reactive person and a proactive person.

When you want to take charge of the direction your life takes and of your future outcomes, there is also only one way to do it: becoming proactive in making the right choices at the right time.

Developing a Bias to Action

If you have been living your life in a reactive role, making the switch to a proactive approach will take a consistent dedication to take charge of what happens in your life. But how do you determine whether you are a reactive personality?

Here are the main characteristics of reactive people.

- You are prone to extreme highs and lows
- You often feel helpless and find it hard to make decisions in your relationships and life in general

- You often try to live up to other people's expectations
- You find it hard to trust and follow your instincts
- You often assign blame to others
- You are resistant to change and prefer the status quo
- You are easily offended

If you have a reactive personality then you may recognize most of the above traits to be consistent with your general disposition. Fortunately, it is possible to adopt a more proactive approach to life that will allow you to make the necessary changes for a better life.

Here are some simple strategies that can take you from reactive to proactive

1) Start with making small decisions

If making huge life changes scares you, start by making small changes that will lead you to the intended goal. If, for example, you want to get away from an abusive relationship, instead of moving out to live on your own, move back home to stay with your family. You have still made the right decision but you will have the support of your family to keep you going until you feel ready to live on your own.

This will help you to get yourself together in a safe space as you consider your next move. Most of the paralysis that holds us back is broken when we make the first step. Whatever the change is that you need to make in your life, start by making small decisions that will eventually get you to your end goal.

2) Do not put off till tomorrow what you can do today.

Do not wait for a perfect moment or time to make your move. Procrastination is simply an avoidance tool used by reactive people. The best time to take charge of your life is now. Most enablers stay caught in the codependency cycle by the constant thought of *this is the last time I am doing it*. By constantly putting off making a decision, they keep enabling the addict until it is too late.

Start now, start where you are and start with what you have. If you keep putting off making changes to your life, you will never free yourself from the vicious cycle of toxic relationships and bad outcomes.

3) Have a timeline

Have a timeline for yourself that holds you accountable. Making open-ended declarations without a timeline will not really have an impact on your life. Real change is bound to a measurable timeline. For instance, there is a world of difference between *I need to lose 15 pounds by next month* and *I need to lose weight.*

The first one communicates a clear intent with an actionable timeline while the second is a simple declaration. The first person is more likely to reach their goal because they are specific about what they want and when they want it.

4) Don't be a perfectionist.

When you pursue perfection, you are likely to get nowhere first. Appreciate your progress even if it takes place in small steps. Every step you make towards changing your life should be celebrated. It is the small victories that will spur you on to make the big changes.

For instance, if all you did today was speak up for yourself, do not be discouraged. Tomorrow you will make another change and another one after that until you are no longer in a toxic relationship.

5. Step out of your comfort zone

You must do something you have never done to get something you have never had. Do not be afraid to venture out of your comfort zone and explore new possibilities. Challenge yourself to confront your fears and see what is on the other side.

Changing your Self-Dialogue

Before your reality can change you must first change your thoughts. It is our thoughts that tell us how far we can go and how high we should aim. If all you think are self-limiting thoughts then your reality will be a reflection of that.

Consider the kind of things you were telling yourself as a codependent, *it is my fault, I just want to help him, she needs me, I cannot abandon him, what if she leaves me* and so on and so forth. All these thoughts were coming from a place of fear, shame, and guilt. They held you captive in a toxic relationship. If you are to successfully find a better life, then these thoughts need to change.

Throughout the day, you talk to yourself in the form of the thoughts you are thinking. You have a running commentary inside your mind and this commentary is what we are referring to as self-dialogue. Have you ever stopped to consider what your self-dialogue sounds like? If you were to say those things out loud to someone else how would they feel?

When we talked about self-empathy, we highlighted the need to be as kind to ourselves as we are to our friends. That is exactly what you need to do with your internal dialogue. *You are ugly..., why are you so stupid..., you never get anything right...,* Would you ever say any of those things to your friend or spouse? Of course not, they are hurtful and mean. So why do you say them to yourself?

When you think of it that way, you realize that we rarely treat ourselves with the same kindness we treat others. If you are to achieve any meaningful change in your life, this kind of self-dialogue has to change. When you start to pay attention to your internal dialogue, then you start to realize all the little ways in which you self-sabotage without even being consciously aware of it.

In the Solomon Islands, when the islanders want to harvest a tree, they do not chop it down with a chainsaw. Instead, they gather around it in groups and yell insults at it. They do this for thirty consecutive days and by the last day, the tree starts to wither and die.

Now, this may be a myth founded in fact or fiction but the power of negativity to drain the life out of a living thing is not debatable. How many things do you talk yourself out of because of fear and other negative emotions? Until you realize the power that your self-dialogue has on you, you will keep self-sabotaging and killing your own dreams.

Simple strategies to silence the nagging voice in your head

a) Challenge your opinions

Counter your negative thoughts with evidence to the contrary. If you catch yourself thinking *I will never amount to anything,* switch your focus to all the things you have done right in your life. Do not be vague be specific about your accomplishments and slowly you will start to uproot the defeatist mentality.

Most of our opinions are based on something that happened once that we then turned into a generalization. If you can find evidence to the contrary, you minimize the hold of that generalization on your thoughts and emotions.

b) If you wouldn't say it to someone else, don't say it to yourself.

135

Practice self-empathy by being kind to yourself. Stop nitpicking and finding things that are wrong with your life. Bolster your confidence by believing in yourself and not being overly critical of your mistakes. Learn to forgive yourself the same way you forgive others and absolve them of guilt and blame.

c) Practice self-affirmation

Use self-affirmation to counter negative self-dialogue. Research has found that positive self-affirmation has a significant impact on feelings of self-worth and confidence. Here are some examples of simple self-affirmation mantras.

- My life is filled with meaning purpose
- I will not sweat the small stuff
- I deserve to be happy
- I am confident, I am accomplished and I am good at what I do
- I am enough
- I will not fail
- I will not give up

d) Recognize your triggers

We all have certain triggers that cause us to think and act a certain way. You may find that being around certain people makes you more negative. This is an indication that you are in a toxic relationship. If someone in your life makes you question your self-worth, it may be time to set up your boundaries. Do not allow people to steal your joy and make you feel inferior or unworthy.

Other triggers can be unresolved issues or traumatic events that happened in the past. Always work to resolve your unresolved issues either by getting professional help or by confronting them on your own. When you let unresolved issues fester, they taint all your thoughts and emotions with negativity.

e) Get rid of thoughts that are not yours

Even in your internal dialogue, you will be surprised to learn that most of the negative thoughts you have were planted by other people. A teacher, a parent a former partner or even friends. Separate your thoughts from external influences that intrude on your emotions and thoughts.

Let other people's opinions be just that; opinions and not the defining thoughts in your mind. The same way you would not consume junk food if you want a healthy body, if you want a healthy mind, watch the kind of information you allow yourself to dwell on.

Set Your Own Goals

Goals give you purpose and something to work toward. If you were in a codependent relationship, chances are you did not have personal goals. You were probably focused on helping the other person meet their needs and paying no attention to yours. But now that you are free of codependency what do you want out of life?

Our sense of self-worth originates from being useful and knowing we are doing something worthwhile with our lives. Figuring out what you want out of life is an important part of getting your life back on track. If you have not thought about it yet. Now is the time to set some goals for your life that will enable you to meet your needs and have an-all round life.

Even when you are in a relationship, you should still keep your personal goals in mind. Everyone needs a purpose and meaning for their life. This cannot be determined by other people or your relationships. Your goals have to come from you. They need to be in alignment with your core values and your passions.

If you are just floating around life with no real sense of purpose, you will be more susceptible to codependency. This is because you will latch on to other people to get some meaning in your life. Remember we mentioned that enablers often help the addict to stay addicted because it gives them a sense of purpose to have someone to care for. If you have your own goals, you will not need anyone else to give your life meaning.

You do not have to have every little detail of your life planned out ahead of time. You just need a general idea of where you want to go and what you need to do to get there. Start with the small goals and build your way up to the bigger ones.

Get into the habit of setting goals for yourself every week. Have a list of things that you want to accomplish that week. They can be personal or professional goals or both. At the end of the week review your goals and see how many you have accomplished. Build up to monthly and long-term goals. Slowly you will find your life becoming more purposeful since you have goals that you are working toward.

Goal-setting strategies

a) Set goals that inspire you to act

the goals you set should motivate you. It is important to have goals that are linked to your passions and needs. When you are looking forward to getting something, doing the work required will be easy.

Avoid setting goals that you would not really care about one way or another. Goals have to be the things that mean a lot to you and have a meaningful impact on your life.

b) Be specific about what you want to achieve

Do not set vague goals. Be as specific as possible down to the timeline for each specific goal you are setting. You need to be able to measure your progress. If you set vague goals, they will not be measurable or bound to an actionable timeframe.

c) Put it down on paper

Goals are more tangible and binding when you actually write them down. The simple act of writing them makes you feel compelled to accomplish them. Think of it as kind of a contract or covenant that you are making with yourself. You need to have a record that you can look back on and say, *this is what I wanted and I managed to do it.*

d) Focus on what you want

Do not set goals like, *I do not want to be broke anymore,* focus on what you want not what you do not want. You can change that to something like, *I want to have a certain amount in savings by the end of the year.*

Positive goals tend to have more power than negative ones. Keep your focus on what you want and what you don't want will take care of itself in the process.

e) Do not give up

Not all of your goals will come to fruition when you want them to. That doesn't mean you should give up. Always be realistic and expect that some things will go the way you want them to and some won't no matter what you do. Keep a positive mindset and always be ready to set new goals and milestones for yourself.

The 21 Day Rule

Habits are hard to break. We get into a certain pattern of thinking and behaving that becomes second nature. This is what makes change so difficult to achieve. For change to occur, we have to discard old destructive habits and replace them with new ones.

To understand how habits are formed, we need to have a look at how the brain functions. Actions that are repeated become habits. For instance, if you wake up at the same time every day, that becomes a habit and you will find yourself repeating it daily without consciously thinking about it.

If you usually have your morning coffee every day at 10 am, you will soon start getting cravings for a cup of coffee every day at the same time. This is the power that habits have on our behavior and actions.

Habits become entrenched after the repeated performance of a certain action or routine. After many repetitions of an act, the brain creates a loop that starts with a certain trigger. This trigger then pushes the brain into autopilot. This principle of the brain creating loops for repeated actions is the reason why practice makes perfect. With each repetition, your brain gets better and better at accomplishing the task.

Habits strengthen the neural pathways in the brain that are associated with a particular action. This strengthening of neural pathways is responsible for habit formation and in extreme cases addiction. Addicts find themselves unable to stop doing something because it has become entrenched in their neural pathways. The loop created in the brain for addiction starts with a trigger that initiates the action, the action itself and then the reward for the action.

Repetition fosters efficiency in the brain cells. When this efficiency is linked to a certain behavior or habit the behavior becomes entrenched and hard to break. For instance, if you are a comfort eater, you are triggered by emotional stress to start eating. Once you eat you feel temporary relief from your anxiety. The more you repeat this habit the more your brain will link stress to comfort eating and the harder it will be to break this habit.

With this in mind, it is important to realize that habits are more than just something you can create on a whim. It takes a lot of consistency and repetition to create new habits and entrench them in such a way that they replace old habits. That is why following the 21-day rule is important.

Research has shown that if you repeat a certain behavior or action consistently every day for at least 21 days you can successfully create a new habit. This means that in the journey to freeing yourself from codependency you should be willing to ditch your old codependency tendencies and adopt new habits.

Effective Strategies for forming new habits.

1. Be consistent

There can be no days off when you give yourself a break when you are trying to form new habits. You have to be consistent and persistent. As we have seen above habit formation is dependent on the repetition of a routine until it becomes entrenched in your brain.

2. Keep yourself motivated

Doing something over and over can be tedious and frankly quite boring. However, if you keep your eye on the reward or what you are hoping to achieve then you will get the motivation to keep going. The process will be worth it in the end if it frees you from self -destructive habits and addictions.

3. Make your environment conducive

Avoid sabotaging your progress by having any triggers removed from your environment. For instance, if you are trying to eat healthier, ensure you remove all junk food from your pantry and refrigerator. Making your environment conducive makes the process easier for you and removes possible temptations from sight.

4. Start your day with the new habit

When you make the new habit the first thing you do in the morning, you are less likely to lose your motivation. In the morning your brain is free of clutter and any pressures that may interfere with your new habit. This will make it easy to follow through on the habit until it becomes entrenched.

5. Pair the habit with something you love to do

For added motivation, pair the new habit with something you love to do to make it more enjoyable and to motivate yourself to keep going. Listen to your favorite podcast as you engage in the activity or get someone to join you on your quest. Making the habit a dull affair will make it harder to follow through. Try and make it enjoyable in some way.

6. Do not try to entrench multiple habits at a time

Start small. Do not make the change more difficult for yourself by trying to change too many things at once. You are more likely to be successful if you take a systematic approach.

7. Get an accountability partner

Let someone close to you know what you are trying to accomplish. This will make you feel accountable and motivate you to persist until you succeed. A good support system can be the difference between you sticking to your goal or giving up.

8. Keep going

There will be days when you do not want to, but you have to remind yourself what you stand to gain if you persevere. Be patient with yourself but also push yourself to get it done. If you fail once, start again and repeat the process until you get it right.

Chapter 10: Codependency Recovery; Your Tools at A Glance

Everyone's story is different. You may be a Jenny who needs just one wake up call to spur them into action or your detangling process may be more gradual. Whatever the case may be, the key thing is arriving at the decision that you can be free of codependency, that you do deserve a better life and you can do better for yourself.

Once you come to this realization, then your battle with codependency is halfway won. In the larger scheme of things, it is not the scars from your past that define you, rather it is the lessons you choose to take away from those scars. Do not be ashamed of your past, wear your experiences with pride and as a sign of just how far you have come.

No journey is ever completely smooth and there are a few universal truths that will help to keep you going. These truths are the tools that you need to carry with you to remind you of just where you are going, what you have freed yourself from and more importantly what you need to keep going.

The trick to real and lasting change is to do it in small and manageable doses. Do not overwhelm yourself with long lists of things you need to do or not do. Pick you struggles one at a time and take them apart one by one. Above all, understand that recovery from codependency is a journey and not a page you can just flip.

Self-Assertion

If you are a play-along to get-along kind of person then you probably do not like conflict. People who shy away from conflict or having to differ with others prefer to just accept other people's opinions even when they do not agree with them. This is especially true for codependents who are natural people-pleasers.

If you have a problem with self-assertion you will often find yourself feeling resentful and angry and not have a clue why that is happening. When you constantly suppress your needs in order to accommodate and please other people, sooner or later the frustration of not having your needs met will start to show.

This frustration will manifest itself in the form of emotional outbursts over petty issues, moodiness, and feelings of resentment toward your partner. None of these feelings are recipes for a good relationship so it turns out that play-along to get-along does not really work in the long term.

The first thing you need to understand is that there is a world of difference between compromising and ignoring your needs. In a compromise situation, you and your partner acknowledge each other's needs and agree to both compromise and meet halfway. Compromise is a healthy part of any relationship. However, when you ignore your needs it means you have not made the other party aware of your needs and you simply choose to focus on their needs. This is the classic trait of many codependents who feel the need to accommodate and people-please.

Self-assertion is being able to clearly articulate your needs and let the other person know how you feel. Being assertive is part of open communication in a relationship. It lets your partner know what you expect from them and also what they can expect from you.

This kind of communication is crucial in building better relationships.

You cannot blame your partner for not meeting your needs when you have not even communicated to them what those needs are. This means that as you recover from codependence, self-assertion is one of the skills that you need to develop.

Assertive communication is built on three main tenets that you need to master. These are:

- Confident communication
- Clear communication
- Controlled communication

These tenets mean that you are able to confidently articulate your needs and get your message across. It also means that your message is clear and to the point with no ambiguity. Finally, your communication is measured and controlled and free of emotional outbursts.

Confidence and clarity are important in making your message understood. When you are confident about what you are saying people tend to take you more seriously because you come across as self-assured and aware of what you want. Control is important because it helps you communicate effectively and objectively without letting emotion take control of you,

When you resort to shouting or yelling to get your point across you are no longer being assertive. Assertiveness is being forthright about your needs but still being accommodating of the other person and giving them a chance to express themselves as well.

When you feel the need to resort to aggressive behavior such as yelling or shouting, it means you feel powerless and are trying to bully the other person rather than communicate with them. It is therefore important to always remember the difference between self-assertion and aggression.

The benefits of being assertive:

- ✓ It helps you to get things done
- ✓ It earns you respect from the other party
- ✓ It makes compromise and conflict resolution easy
- ✓ It makes you less prone to anxiety and stress

Being assertive is not just better for your relationships, but it also makes you more confident. If you struggle with being self-assertive here are some simple strategies you can use to become more assertive.

1. Use I statements

You want to be assertive and not aggressive therefore focus on I statements like, *I feel... or I think... or I need you to....* Avoid aggressive statements such as, *you never..., you should..., you must....*

I statements are a good way to get your point across without coming off as aggressive or accusatory.

2. Keep it simple

Be simple and direct, avoid beating about the bush and get straight to the point. If you speak in circles, people have a hard time understanding what you mean.

3. Expect differences

People are entitled to their own views and they do not have to accept your point of view. Respect other people's opinions even if they differ from yours. Respect is usually a two-way street. If you are respectful, people will also extend you the same courtesy.

4. Stay calm

Kee your composure even when you are not getting the response you wanted or expected. At the end of the day letting your emotions drive you to overreacting will only undermine your message.

Being Your Own Best Friend

Recovering from codependency is only possible if you are able to establish healthy self-esteem and a sense of self-worth. We discussed in length how low self-esteem predisposes people to codependency. A person with a low sense of self-worth will naturally seek to get their validation from the other people in their lives.

This is what fosters codependency habits such as enabling, caretaking and many more. If you are to escape the trap of codependency, the first place you need to look is inward. A healthy self-esteem will solve most of the insecurities and fears that lead to the development of codependency in the first place.

Fears like the fear of rejection and the fear of abandonment are all stoked by low self-esteem. To fight these fears, you need to cultivate a sense of safety and security that is tied to your own self worth and not to other people. This will free you from the need to seek validation and approval from others.

When it comes to building self-esteem, this is pretty much an inside job that depends on your ability to change your opinion of yourself. This change is only possible if you learn to practice self-empathy and become your own best cheerleader.

Consider how you treat your friends. You compliment them, buy them gifts on their birthday, support them when they need you and help them celebrate their victories. You defend them from other people and feel protective over them. This is completely natural and healthy for a good relationship.

However, how many of those things do you do for yourself? do you celebrate your victories? are you protective of your boundaries, do you compliment yourself? Chances are you do not do any of these things for yourself. This is because while we are taught from a young age to be considerate of others, no one ever really teaches us to be kind to ourselves.

Being your own best friend means being considerate of your needs, and taking care of your emotional and psychological health. It means being kind to yourself and forgiving yourself for your past mistakes. Only when you are able to do this can you start to rebuild your self-esteem.

We often carry with us scars that were inflicted as early as childhood without giving ourselves permission to let go and move on. Self-empathy requires you to be willing to accept your flaws and forgive yourself for mistakes you may have made in the past.

There is nothing selfish about being your own best friend, it simply means that you choose to love and celebrate who you are. It frees you from the burden of trying to seek validation in other people or relationships.

Here are simple tips that will help you practice self-love and being your own best friend.

a) Spend time doing the things you love

Make time for your passions and the things that make you truly happy. Do not feel guilty about wanting some time to yourself to do something you love.

b) Get rid of negative energy

Free yourself from people who are always dragging you down and stealing your joy. Be selective about who you allow into your inner circle and life. Be ruthless when it comes to safeguarding your inner peace.

c) Focus on the positive

Don't be your biggest critic. Focus on the things you love about yourself and accept your flaws as just a normal part of human nature. No one is perfect and constantly focusing on your weaknesses will only undermine your confidence.

d) Take care of your body

Stay healthy and active. A healthy body builds your confidence and self-esteem. Take time to exercise and eat well. You only get one body in this life so take care of it. Avoid over-indulging in unhealthy habits that damage your health in the long run.

e) Stay true to your values

Keep your values close at heart and make decisions that are in line with your core values. Your values will help you to make better choices and to avoid following trends and other people's opinions just to please others.

Saying No to Toxic Relationships

Perhaps one of the more challenging aspects of codependent tendencies is the tendency to soak up other people's distress. When you do not have sufficient boundaries to safeguard your emotions. You end up making other people's problems your own. This effectively leads you to a codependent situation where you are unable to separate yourself from the other person.

Such toxic relationships bring out the worst in you because the other person knows exactly what buttons to push to get you to toe the line. You will find yourself often doing things you would otherwise never consider doing just to keep the other person happy. This dysfunction if left unchecked becomes a self-repeating cycle that takes over your life.

Toxic relationships poison you from the inside out. In extreme cases, they may even drive you to coping mechanisms such as addictions to help you process your unresolved issues. This potential for self-harm is one of the reasons why freeing yourself from codependency requires that you eliminate any toxic relationships from your life.

Whether you are dealing with a narcissist who thrives on attention and being the center of the universe, or with more covert manipulators, the damage to your self-esteem is hard to repair.

Toxic people will come in many different shapes and forms and you need to be able to identify them by their characteristics.

Here are some of the warnings signs that you need to be on the lookout for if you are to identify toxic people and weed them out.

- ✓ They like to control you
- ✓ They like to shift blame and never take responsibility for their actions
- ✓ They are overly critical and always trying to find fault
- ✓ They use threats and intimidation to manipulate you.
- ✓ They try to gain sympathy by playing
- ✓ They are always complaining
- ✓ They often use emotional abuse to make you feel worthless.

Perhaps the most toxic relationship for a codependent is one with a narcissist. Narcissists have no consideration or interest in other people's feelings or needs. When it comes to empathy and compassion, the narcissist is the polar opposite of the codependent.

Here are the classic signs that point to a narcissistic personality.

- They lack empathy and never try to meet your needs
- They manipulate you to get what they want
- They expect you to cater to their every need and whim without question
- They demand to have the best of everything
- They are constantly making you feel inferior
- They have a compulsive need to be the center of attention.

Tips for freeing yourself from toxic relationships

1) Build boundaries

Identify your limits and do not compromise on your boundaries. Be very clear on what is and isn't acceptable. Always be ready to enforce the consequence of the other person crossing your boundaries. This means you should be ready to cut off ties with this person permanently if they are unwilling to change.

2) Stop taking responsibility for other people's problems.

The only person whose happiness you are responsible for is you. Stop trying to fix other people's problems. Never feel obligated to rescue or support someone who is unwilling to take responsibility for their actions.

By trying to fix the other person's problems you become an enabler and promote dysfunction and codependence in the relationship. People tend to become more conscientious when they know that they will be responsible for the consequences of their actions.

3) Discover your triggers

Identify the triggers that make you vulnerable to manipulation. Whether you have unresolved issues with guilt, blame or shame, know what your triggers are. Be vigilant around anyone trying to use these triggers against you. For instance, someone trying to guilt you into doing something you do not want is exploiting your guilt issues.

4) Build your emotional intelligence

Emotional intelligence enables you to manage your emotions effectively. It allows you to stop being reactive to other people and have more control over your behavior and feelings

Emotional intelligence also increases your social awareness and the ability to recognize other people's motives. This makes it easier for you to spot manipulators and energy vampires and give them a wide berth.

5) Find safety and security in yourself

When you are secure in yourself, you no longer feel the need to be validated or approved by others. This leaves you free to make decisions based on your needs. Freedom from the need for validation also means that you no longer have to try and please others to feel loved or accepted. This frees you up to be true to yourself without fretting about other people's opinions.

6) Surround yourself with positive people

When you build healthy relationships, you will be less likely to get back into dysfunctional relationships. Focus on making new emotional connections with people who share your values. A good relationship will help you get over a bad one that much faster. It will also give you a chance to experience what a good relationship should be.

Knowing Which Walls to Build

When you think of walls, you immediately think of protection and safeguarding something. That is exactly what walls do in your emotional life as well. They keep the good stuff in and safeguard you from the negative. That is why you need to build walls around the things you need to keep protected.

Your values, your self-esteem, your interests, and your goals are some of the things that you need to protect at all costs. When you are in a codependent state, these pieces of you get lost in the relationship as you put all your energy into meeting the needs of the other person. In that case, you get lost in the relationship and lack any sense of self-worth or individuality.

To avoid falling into this trap, walls help you to create boundaries that set limits for your self and the people in your life. These walls say to you and the people in your life that these are things that I will not compromise on. Retaining your values, passions, and interests is important in the journey of recovery from codependency.

In effect walls are the boundaries you create to preserve your sense of self. The last thing you want is for your self-worth to be tied up in your relationship. Making your relationship your entire life is not only a recipe for disaster but it also makes you more vulnerable to slipping back into the role of a codependent.

Remember that when you lack boundaries you leave yourself open to abuse and manipulation. It is only by knowing where you stop and the other person begins that you can hope to have a healthy and balanced relationship.

When it comes to healthy boundaries, apart from setting your own you need to respect the walls other people have put up. Codependents typically over function in the other person's life meaning they will often cross the boundary of what is acceptable. Tendencies like tracking their partner's every move are common codependent characteristics.

The same way you need others to respect your boundaries you have to be aware of where other people's limits are. The best way to avoid getting too involved in some else life is to have a life of your own. Have goals, interests, and hobbies to keep you involved in your own life and out of other people's business.

Have enough confidence and trust in your relationship that you do stifle or smother the other person due to insecurities. People thrive in relationships where they do not feel trapped by an overzealous partner.

However even as you build boundaries do not shy away from intimate connections and meaningful relationships. It is common for people who are recovering from codependency to be wary of relationships because of a fear of slipping back into old patterns.

Do not deny yourself a chance at happiness by avoiding intimate emotional connections. Trust yourself to have a healthy relationship that is not influenced by your past mistakes or impacted by unresolved issues. Healthy boundaries are key to recovery from codependency but do not self-isolate from relationships and love as a defense from getting hurt.

Tips for building better boundaries

1) Identify your limits

Identify what you want to protect and where essentially your limits are. Decide what you are willing to compromise on and what is a deal-breaker for you. You can base these decisions on your values and the things that are important to you.

2) Be assertive

Communicate your boundaries clearly and let the other person know what you expect from them and what they can expect from you. That way both parties are fully aware of what they are getting into and are fully prepared for it.

3) Cultivate self-awareness

The only way to set good boundaries is to understand yourself first. When you appreciate what your needs are, you can set reasonable boundaries that will help you meet your needs.

4) Consider your unresolved issues

Only you can know where your triggers and weaknesses are. Set boundaries that will help you cope with these weaknesses and make it easy for you to escape the traps that made you codependent in the first place.

5) Prioritize your needs

Boundaries should be about ensuring that whichever relationship you are getting into, your needs are being met. This means that your primary consideration when setting limits should be your needs and what you want from the relationship.

Embracing Healthy Relationships

You have worked hard to free yourself from toxic relationships. The last thing you want is to fall back into the trap of codependency. So how do you ensure that your relationships are healthy and emotionally balanced? What are the signs that the relationship you are getting into is not another dysfunctional relationship in the making?

The first thing to do when looking to embrace healthy relationships is identifying what you want in a relationship. These are all the things that make a healthy relationship.

a) Open communication

In a healthy relationship, both parties are free to express themselves freely without fear of judgment. If you feel safe enough to open up to your partner and express your emotions and needs then your relationship is healthy.

Open communication creates a safe space for both parties in the relationship to be heard and understood. There is mutual give and take in this kind of relationship. You have no trouble articulating your needs or understanding your partner's needs.

b) You have a life

In a healthy relationship, you still retain your individuality. You have your own goals, interest, and passions. This means that your self-worth is internal and not dependent on your partner. You are confidently pursuing your own goals and sharing your experiences with your partner. The relationship is important to you but it is not the only thing in your life.

c) You have healthy boundaries

You never feel the need to solve your partner's problems because he takes responsibility for his own actions. You are both aware of each other's needs but respect each other space. Your relationship is built on mutual balance and both parties meet each other halfway. No one feels compelled to over function in the other person's life.

d) You are not constantly seeking approval from your partner

You have healthy self-esteem and you do not rely on your partner to validate or affirm you. Your sense of security lies within and you are not constantly trying to please your partner.

e) You compromise

In a healthy relationship, you and your partner can resolve conflicts amicably and reach a suitable compromise for both parties. You do not feel the need to suppress your emotions or blindly follow what the other person is saying. You can disagree respectfully without getting emotional or aggressive.

f) You have fun

Your relationship is not full of anxiety or jealousy or insecurity. You have fun together and enjoy each other's company. No one feels pressured to keep reassuring the other because you both have high self-esteem and confidence in yourselves.

Along with all the things that you want in a healthy and balanced relationship, there are also plenty that you want to avoid. When recovering from codependency you want to avoid relationships that set off your old triggers. You can easily slip black into a dysfunctional relationship if you do not guard against toxic relationships.

Always remember that narcissists are masters of manipulation and they can easily exploit your weaknesses to set you back to a codependent cycle. Trust your instincts and always go with your gut. If your gut warns you that someone is not right for you, trust your sixth sense and avoid getting emotionally involved with that person.

Ultimately narcissists and energy vampires come in different shapes and forms and you will sometimes have to rely on your judgment to suss out potentially harmful relationships. However, there are still classic signs of things that you do not want in your relationship. When you see any of these red flags, remove yourself from the situation immediately.

Here are the red flags to keep a lookout for when embracing healthy relationships.

a) You often feel anxious and stressed

If you are in a relationship and you are often stressed out, this is a sign that your needs are not being met. This is typically a result of you either not articulating them properly or having a partner who is ignoring your needs.

The only relationships worth pursuing are the ones that make you happy. If your relationship is making you stressed and anxious, it may be time to reconsider your choices.

b) You often have to cancel your plans to accommodate the other person

This is another classic red flag to watch out for. Compromise is a normal part of any relationship. However, if you are the only one who constantly has to sacrifice their needs to keep the other person happy, chances are that you are being manipulated.

If you are not being assertive about your needs, the constant self-sacrifice will turn into resentment and anger which will ultimately undermine the relationship. Be assertive enough to say no when you need to. Do not feel like you have to accommodate the other person's needs at your expense.

c) Your life revolves around the other person

If you are constantly just sitting around waiting for your partner to come home. Then you have over-invested yourself in their relationship and are risking getting into a codependent cycle.

If you are constantly thinking and worrying about your partner, you do not have a life of your own outside of the relationship. This is also a predisposing factor for the development of codependency and dysfunctional attachment.

d) You are doing things for your partner that he should be doing himself

When you start taking up the roles of the other person, it shows that they are no healthy boundaries in your relationship. This leaves you open to abuse and manipulation. In a healthy relationship, each person takes up their respective responsibilities.

e) You often feel guilty or ashamed

If you are constantly being guilted or shamed into doing things that you do not want to, then you are setting yourself up to fail. Only manipulative and narcissistic people will use triggers such as shame and guilt to get what they want from you.

Ultimately, the health of your relationship will be dependent on the health of your emotional state going into it. Leave your emotional baggage outside the door and release yourself from unresolved issues from your past if you want to enjoy truly deep and meaningful emotional connections in your relationship.

Conclusion

Codependent No More was intended to provide people struggling with codependency and dysfunctional relationships with a lifeline that they can use to stop the cycle of toxic relationships. The recovery process for codependency, just like any other condition, starts with self-awareness. By taking the step to learn more about this condition you have already made the decision to release yourself from the cycle of codependency.

Struggling with creating healthy relationships can have a big impact on the quality of your life and your emotional state. We are created as social beings who thrive on intimacy and deep emotional connections. Ensuring that your relationships are healthy and balanced is, therefore, a key consideration for most people who want to change their outcomes and live better lives.

Often, when we cannot identify or diagnose our emotional needs, it becomes difficult to form healthy relationships. Since you have taken some insights from this book on what may be causing your emotional dependency, you are now fully empowered to face the issue head-on. You have the opportunity to build relationships that are fulfilling and meaningful and best of all free of codependency. Toxic relationships can be a thing of the past for you if you are willing to put into practice the techniques you have picked up in this book.

Knowledge is one of the most effective weapons against codependency because once you know what triggers to look out for, the rest is just a matter of finding the will and the dedication to follow through on your recovery process. Remember that with consistent application of the techniques that you have learned in this book you can successfully overcome codependency and embrace healthy relationships.

Challenge yourself to make small changes every day that will help you to break the bad habits that have held you hostage over the years. Once you say no to bad habits, you create room for better habits that can significantly change your life for the better.

Small victories are better than none, so do not be afraid of starting small. Challenge yourself to start your recovery process today. Invest in a better life by choosing to empower and free yourself with the techniques and strategies you have learned in this book.

The aim of this practical guide was to inform, engage and empower you to achieve your goals. Every care was taken to ensure that this book is as informative and useful as possible. We hope it has provided you with all the tools you need to break free of codependency.

Made in the USA
Columbia, SC
09 November 2020

24217871R00095